Thérèse and The Little Way of Love and Healing

John O'Brien OFM

Publisher: Bro. John

2nd Edition

"You pass by a little child, you pass by spitefully, with foul language and a wrathful heart; you may not have noticed the child, but he has seen you, and your face, ugly and profane, will perhaps remain in his defenceless heart. You may not know it, but you have perhaps sown an evil seed in him and it may grow, and all because you did not exercise sufficient care before a child, because you did not foster in yourself a discreet, active love."

– The monk Zossima in *The Brothers Karamazov*
by Fydor Dostoyevsky

This book is dedicated to
Shaun Edwards who has always been a good friend
and Jacqueline Corkish whose idea this book was
and who put in a lot of work with the manuscript

Contents

List of Abbreviations used

CGI, CGII Correspondance Générale, 1972-1973, 2 Volumes, French

CSG Conseils et souvenirs, Soeur Geneviève, (Céline), Conseils et souvenirs, Paris, Éd du Cerf, 1952, 1973 & 1989

DE Derniers Entretiens

EC Conférences of Sr. Marie-Eugene

GCII General correspondence, Volume 2, 1988, English translation by John Clarke, OCD

LT Letters written by Thérèse, translated by John Clark

MsA Autobiographical manuscript dedicated to Mother Agnes of Jesus, 1896

MsB Letter to Sr. Marie of the The Sacred Heart, autobiographical manuscript, 1896

MsC Autobiographical manuscript dedicated to Mother Marie de Gonzague, 1897

NPPO Notes préparatoires pour le Procès de l'Ordinaire

PA Procès Apostolique, 1915-1917, Rome, 1976

PN New Poetry classification established in the 1979 French centenary edition

PO Procès Apostolique, 1910-1911, Rome, 1973

RP Théâtre au Carmel: Récréations Pieuses de St. Thérèse de L'Enfant-Jésus, 1985

SS Story of A Soul, 1976, English translation by John Clarke, OCD

St., Sts. Saint/Sainte(s)

Sza., Szas. Stanza(s)

TDNT Theological Dictionary of the New Testament

VVT Verse

VT vie Thérésienne

Acknowledgements

Jacqueline Corkish asked me to write this book to help people find Thérèse's little way. She saw this "little way" as a way of healing and hope. I would like to thank Lydia Corbett (formerly Sylvette David) who painted the cover picture. Lydia was Picasso's muse for "the young girl with a ponytail" series. The back cover is from a stained glass window by George Walsh in Ballynarry church. I would also like to thank Ann-Marie Rooney for all her help and work with the manuscript.

Introduction

St. Thérèse used to make many little comments to those she was close to. Her desire to become a priest is well recorded - but maybe not the reasons. She used to hear so many sermons, especially on Mary, that she reckoned she could do better! She, herself, after death would suffer the fate of a million bad sermons. Thérèse had a lovely sense of humour - she was a great mimic and would entertain the sisters with her mimicking of the preachers who came to Lisieux. These facts alone make me proceed with caution - I am aware of Thérèse and her wry views.

Thérèse was not given to over-sentimentality. When she arrived at a decision - she was deadly in earnest. She described her vocation as being love in the heart of the church. She would be this heart of love. This vocation is also very prophetic. In the world in which we live, the heart of love is sadly often not to be found. Thérèse would embrace this heart of love in a world where the heart of darkness reigns. Thérèse's prayer, faith and life became a living statement that this heart is not the one that will conquer in the end. Thérèse also had a prophetic vision that others would follow her 'little way' of love and bring this love into our world. This is what she prayed for (see MsB, 5v°). Mother Teresa of Calcutta (d. 1997) spoke of the suffering of this world. It is the suffering of loneliness and it is the disease of our modern world. This was the place where she saw need of those who live the 'heart of love' in our world. Mother Teresa was born Agnes Gonxha Bojaxhiu (26th August, 1910). Gonxha means 'little flower' in Albanian. This is the name given to Thérèse. Both women saw a wounded world and sought to bring light and healing to this world by their lives.

In my own life, I have experienced - for a long time - the effects of the heart of darkness of this world. It did not destroy my faith but I know, intimately, the pain of rejection, the sick, hopeless feelings that follow abuse, and the pain of feeling isolated and unwanted. St. John of The Cross says:

> "In other sicknesses, following sound philosophy, contraries are cured by contraries, but love is incurable except by things in accord with love. The reason for this is that the love of God is the soul's health and the soul does not have full health until love is complete"
>
> (Spiritual Canticle, 11. 11).

Thérèse's life and her little way is a journey to this love and it is a way of allowing this love - the love that God has for us - become the life of the soul. In the measure that loves grows, the healthier we become. Thérèse's life and her doctrine of the little way always has been a source of healing for me. This is the journey I share in this work. She leads us to healing and asks us to become healers of others.

St. John of The Cross tells us:

> "...love of God is the soul's health and the soul does not have full health until love is complete. Sickness is nothing but the lack of health, and when the soul has not even a single degree of love she is dead. But when she possesses some degrees of love of God, no matter how few, she is then alive, yet very weak and infirm because of her little love. In the measure that love increases she will be healthier, and when love is perfect she will have full health."
>
> (Spiritual Canticle, 12.11)

The World Health Organisation produced the 'International Classification of Impairments, Disabilities and Handicaps' in 1980 (which was later modified in 1997). The document refers to four strata of illness. There is, firstly, pathology which relates to abnormalities or failure in the function of an organ or organ system; secondly, there is impairment which refers to abnormalities or changes in the function of the whole body. Then there is a reduction in activity which relates to abnormalities, changes or restrictions in the interaction between a person and her or his environment or physical context; and, finally, there is the question of participation. This relates to change, limitations or abnormalities in the position of the person in their social context.

The human heart thirsts for love and the heart that is not loved dies. When the heart is wounded by a lack of love, it fulfils the modern definition of illness. The person suffers impairment in interaction, his or her activity is reduced and the person is unable to participate with others. There we see how modern John of The Cross is. The fullness of love is found in God Who is Love itself and as we enter, by the grace of The Holy Spirit, into the heart of God's love, we become healthy and "when love is perfect " the soul (she) "will have full health ".

The way to this love is Jesus Who is "The Way, The Truth and The Life" (Jn. 14:6). Jesus was fully human: - he had a heart that desired to be accepted and loved. He desired to love and be loved.

The Letter to the Hebrews reminds us that:

> "It was necessary that He should in this way be made completely like his brothers and sisters so that He could become a compassionate and trustworthy high priest for their relationship to God, able to expiate the sins of the people. For the suffering He Himself passed through while being put to the test enabled him to help others when they are being put to the test".
>
> (Heb. 2:17-18).

Jesus lived in solidarity with the broken-hearted. In being fully human, Jesus lived in a world where it is impossible to be fully human without undergoing suffering. Ultimately, this led to his cross. Yet by the power of the Holy Spirit, Jesus rose from the dead and is present to us by the power of the same Holy Spirit. His life points us to the humanity that lies hidden in us all. Yet this is where many are most afraid. Many of us have experienced rejection – to reject someone is to totally wound the heart of the person. In such 'darkness' it is hard to believe that one is loved.

In Georges Bernanos's book 'Nouvelle Histoire de Mouchette' (1937), he tells the story of Mouchette (literally, 'little fly') who was born to a cruel and alcoholic father. She is bullied at school by both teachers and pupils. She is abused as a young girl. At the end of the book she takes her life. Georges Bernanos did not call her death 'suicide'. He said that Mouchette fell asleep, reaching out for the hand of help and love that never came.

Robert Bresson, the French film producer, who is important in the history of film and influenced people like Scorcese, made a film of Bernanos' book called, simply, 'Mouchette' (1967). His portrayal of the lonely Mouchette who is all alone in the cruel world is infinitely sad. Bresson said that Mouchette is to be found everywhere – in prisons, concentration camps, torture chambers and wherever people are cruel to one another.

In Bresson's film when Mouchette dies we hear Monteverdi's Magnificat. When Mouchette reached out for help, no help came from any human - yet the playing of the Magnificat lets us know she is held by God's love. She finds the tenderness she missed in life.

Yet God calls different people to make present The Heart of Love of God revealed in Jesus. Such a person was Thérèse of Lisieux. When Bernanos wrote his work on Mouchette, he saw Mouchette as a Thérèse who was born into a world without love. Bernanos made the point that it is easier than one thinks not to love oneself. This is the world of Mouchette.

Thérèse was born into a loving family. However, she lost her mother at an early age. She then lost her second mother, Pauline, who entered the Carmel at Lisieux. Thérèse fell ill and the doctor feared for her life. She had an experience of love from the smile of The Blessed Virgin that healed her. She would suffer from scruples and was set on a journey of healing when she called on her deceased brothers and sisters to pray for her in Heaven.

In this book, I go on a healing journey with Thérèse. In the first part, I chart the outline of her life and teaching. In the second part, I show her interior journey to her 'little way'. Her little way consists of abandonment. This is her act of accepting the love of God which is infinite. It takes courage to accept acceptance, to accept we are loved unconditionally – it takes courage because we have so often experienced the opposite. The little way consists in living with our smallness and imperfections.

Jesus is The One who lifts us up.

Thérèse uses the metaphor of the 'escalator' or the 'little bird' to describe how The Love of God revealed in Jesus raises us up to The Heart of God. She trusts in his love and mercy.

Her journey is a source of healing in a number of ways. She points us to where health lies. Her inner journey shows how she began to overcome the separation anxiety she experienced when her mother died and Pauline (and, afterwards, Marie) entered Carmel. She also shows how she overcomes her scrupulous nature. In the face of the scruples which tormented her, she came to know the mercy and love of God.

By joining Thérèse on this journey, she helps us to know ourselves, our weaknesses. She helps us to see the hurt rejections have left in us. She gives us courage to discover The Love of God revealed in Jesus and she gives us courage to give ourselves, in faith, to this Love. This is her doctrine of abandonment and of confidence.

Also, Thérèse promised to continue her intercession for us after her death (DE 6-17-1). Thérèse began her work of intercession for the murderer Pranzini, in 1887. Pranzini's case was much discussed in France. This case brought out the worst in people (see Bro, Thérèse of Lisieux, p. 135-141). It brought out the best in Thérèse. Louis, her father, tried to protect his young girls but there was no way they could escape the poisoned atmosphere of France at the time. Thérèse interceded for Pranzini and she read in La Croix (a French, Catholic newspaper) of September 1st, 1887, how Pranzini had kissed the cross on his way to his execution. Guy Gaucher, showed in his work of 2003, "Je voudrais parcourir la terre …", how many people have been helped by Thérèse's prayers. There are many testimonies from a wide range of people.

We find our health in God's love.

In a letter to her favourite sister, Céline, Thérèse says "let us love our bitterness" (LT197)
and "it suffices to humble oneself, to bear with one's imperfections. That is real sanctity " (LT 243, also MsC, 2v°).

Many of us are trained not to love ourselves because of our imperfections. Thérèse lived in a society that was influenced by a movement called Jansenism which had a negative view of humanity and its state. There seemed to be no love for the weak and imperfect. Thérèse short-circuited this movement and enables us to live with ourselves as we become beacons of light and love to help others … to be the ones who help the 'Mouchettes' of our world.

Part One:

Meeting Thérèse

Chapter One

The Two Hearts

"The light shines in the darkness,
and the darkness did not overcome it"   (John 1:5)

When we philosophise or try to explain the "Heart of Darkness", all our efforts appear hollow in the face of a world that is often dark. Yet the works of literature, the world of art and film can communicate better to us than any simplistic formula.

At the end of Hitchcock's film Psycho (1960), we hear the psychiatrist give a scientific, cold description of Norman Bates and why he did what he did. Then the camera pans to Norman who says he wouldn't hurt a fly. Then we see an image of Bates' dead mother and then the images of the people he murdered flicker before us. The images are greater than the psychiatrists reasonable explanation.

Next we meet an Italian film-maker who longed to experience the 'heart of love' of Jesus and Thérèse. He experienced darkness. His name was Pier Paulo Pasolini.

Pier Paolo Pasolini was a man of immense contradictions and was subject to violent passions. He was at once a communist and a Catholic, artist and ideologue, celebrity and outcast, homosexual and rigid traditionalist. One of his earliest poems, "The Ashes of Gramsci" (1954) says

"The scandal, of contradicting myself, of being
with you and against you: with you in my heart.
In light, but against you in the dark viscera."
(cited by Bach, in Sawyer, 2008)

Pasolini was conflicted. He longed to find Jesus, the light and be with him. He longed for a church where Jesus would be made present in love. The world and the church he found were sad and lonely places for him. His art was film-making and he hoped to use his art to express his vision and influence change.

Two of his earlier films, "Medea" and "Oedipus Rex" show his desire to challenge society in post-war Italy. He saw film as a cultural medium that would retrieve the poor from being pushed to the edge of social and cultural oblivion.

He made "Il vangelo secondo Matteo" ("The Gospel According to St. Matthew") in 1964. He did not feel bound to the original Holy Land for his film. He was disappointed by Israel as a movie set. Returning to Rome he decided to shoot "Il vangelo" in southern Italy. His Bethlehem was a village in Apulia, where some people lived in caves. Jerusalem was the crumbling fort of Matera. The desert where Jesus walks is actually in Calabria. He uses local people as extras. Margherita Caruso plays the figure of the young Mary and she appears as one of the ordinary people of the time. There is no hint of her being extraordinary - there are no special effects. She seems ordinary, yet her face shows an inner beauty. Pasolini saw Jesus as the greatest revolutionary of all time. He considered casting Jack Kerouac or Allen Ginsberg in the role. He changed his mind when he met Enrique Irazoqui. In the film Jesus begins teaching along a rocky, barren coastline. He has come to bring a sword not peace. His parables are a call to change and he comes into conflict with the powers that be. So they conspire to have him arrested, beaten, tried and crucified - just as he told his followers.

Pasolini said that for the Roman soldiers at Jesus' preaching in Jerusalem he had to think of the 'celere' (the riot police). For Herod's soldiers before the massacre of the innocents he thought of the Fascist mobs. The figure of Joseph and the Madonna as refugees were suggested to him by analogous tragedies in the world in which he lived. He remembered the trouble in Algeria. Pasolini's Jesus is a very human figure. When Jesus heals the leper there is a beautiful and warm exchange of smiles between him and the man. When Jesus cures the cripple he is overjoyed to see the man come back to him. His smile shows his delight and love.

This was the Jesus Pasolini hoped he would meet in the church. This did not happen and in 1975 Pasolini lost his life in sad circumstances. I understand something of what Pasolini tried to say. Our world of consumerism has made our world less human. Our lonely hearts need to feel the healing touch of Jesus - like Pasolini showed in his film.

The heart of darkness that is in the world and in each of us sometimes appears more real than the heart of love that is in Jesus. In a world of indifference, callousness and abuse the look of love Jesus can appear to be remote and the ultimate reality can seem to be the heart of darkness that manifests itself in cruelty and indifference.

The Heart of Darkness

Joseph Conrad was born Jósef Teodor Konrad Korzeniowski in Poland in 1857. He had an exciting life, including a period in the Belgium Congo in the 1890's. He saw the exploitation of the people and the taking of ivory for sale. This exploitation has not ended. In the second world war uranium used for the atomic bombs came from the same area. In our world today the minerals needed for our computers, lap-tops, iPods, etc., comes, to a large extent from this area also. Many of us in the West do not think about the terrible bloodshed that is taking place there now or in the past. In his book 'The Heart of Darkness' Conrad tells the story of a French gunboat shooting at the local inhabitants indiscriminately. This scene is prophetic - it continues today in different countries. The local people are just natives and are not treated as human beings.

The book is a disturbing work. It concerns a trip by Marlow to a company station which is run by a man called Kurtz. Kurtz has become a leader of the natives and they consider him a demi-god. He is violent and doesn't fit in any more with civilised society, which as the gunboat shows us, is even more violent than Kurtz.

Marlow's journey to Kurtz becomes a journey into himself. The first thing he begins to question - does darkness have a heart? The heart of darkness is hollow and empty. It is hard and callous. Marlow even uses the word 'shadow' to describe Kurtz - Kurtz represents the dark side of Marlow's character. When he meets Kurtz he gives us the following description:

> They only showed that Mr Kurtz lacked restraint in the gratification of his various lusts, that there was something wanting in him - some small matter which, when the pressing need arose, could not be found under his magnificent eloquence. Whether he knew of this deficiency himself I can't say. I think the knowledge came to him at the very last. But the wilderness had found him out early, and had taken on him a terrible vengeance for the fantastic

invasion. I think it had whispered to him things about himself which he did not know, things of which he had no conception till he took counsel with great solitude - and the whisper had proved irresistibly fascinating. It echoed loudly within him because he was hollow at the core.

The symbolic association of the ivory with the heads outside Kurtz's house is then extended until it suggests the very essence of Kurtz himself; Marlow's first description of the man neatly combines the two images:

> I could see the cage of his ribs all astir, the bones of his arms waving. It was as though an animated image of death carved out of old ivory had been shaking its hand with menaces at a motionless crowd of men made of dark and glittering bronze. I saw him open his mouth wide - it gave him a weirdly voracious aspect, as though he had wanted to swallow all the air, all the earth, all the men before him.

Kurtz is a darkness that must be resisted, but this requires an inner journey as well.

Kurtz is ill and tries to escape Marlow and the others and go back into the 'darkness' of the jungle. His heart is somehow in communion with the heart of darkness that exists in our world.

As Marlow blindly searches the jungles, recognising (perhaps a bit conveniently) that he is confusing the beating of drums with that of his heart, he comes upon an ill and desperate Kurtz crawling back toward the savage enclave of which he is the adored leader. This ultimate struggle of will between Marlow and Kurtz can easily be misunderstood. Jocelyn Baines, for instance, asserts that Marlow "is even able to wrest Kurtz from the grasp of the wilderness when he is drawn back to it," which greatly oversimplifies the scene. Marlow does make the statement ("You will be lost . . . Utterly lost") that sways Kurtz in his tortured conflict, but it is Kurtz alone who finally resists the virtually irresistible call of the darkness, and allows himself to be led back to "civilization." Had he chosen to "make a row," Kurtz would have been heard, and rescued, by the natives. But he does not do so, and this is perhaps the basis of his final triumph, and of Marlow's fidelity to his memory.

In his description of their struggle, Marlow gives us the key to the puzzling and terrifying character of Kurtz. The use of the word 'nigger' shows the contempt of Kurtz and the colonials for the local people who were created as less than human.

I had to deal with a being to whom I could not appeal in the name of anything high or low. I had, even like the niggers, to invoke him - himself - his own exalted and incredible degradation. There was nothing either above or below him, and I knew it. He had kicked himself loose of the earth. Confound the man! He had kicked the very earth to pieces. He was alone, and I before him did not know whether I stood on the ground or floated in the air. I've been telling you what we said - repeating the phrases we pronounced - but what's the good? They were common everyday words - the familiar, vague sounds exchanged on every waking day of life. But what of that? They had behind them, to my mind, the terrific suggestiveness of words heard in dreams, of phrases spoken in nightmares. Soul! If anybody has ever struggled with a soul, I am the man. And I wasn't arguing with a lunatic either. Believe me or not, his intelligence was perfectly clear - concentrated, it is true, upon himself with horrible intensity, yet clear; and therein was my only chance - barring of course, the killing there and then, which wasn't so good, on account of the unavoidable noise. But his soul was mad. Being alone in the wilderness, it had looked within itself, and, by heavens! I tell you, it had gone mad. I had - for my sins, I suppose - to go through the ordeal of looking into it myself. No eloquence could have been so withering to one's belief in mankind as his final burst of sincerity. He struggled with himself, too. I saw it, - I heard it. I saw the inconceivable mystery of a soul that knew no restraint, no faith, and no fear, yet struggling blindly with itself.

Several phrases early in the passage - "a being to whom I could not appeal in the name of anything high or low," "There was nothing either above or below him," "He had kicked himself loose from the earth," and particularly, "He was alone" - suggest that Kurtz cannot be taken simply as a symbol of transcendental evil; it is now clear that Kurtz's fate is of general interest because it is a consequence of his isolation, of his absolute freedom. He is a fully autonomous man, attempting to generate and enact his own moral truths, confronting the results of his freedom. In this passage we find the germinal "idea" of the story (to which Conrad had referred in his letter to Cunninghame Graham) most clearly embodied: that "safety" and "value" are illusions that can only be generated and preserved within a given society, while any attempt to place oneself outside these artificial, but necessary, moral structures will drive any man into a perilous condition of "excited imagination." The manager of the Central Station and the other "fools" of the story can never descend to the "heart of darkness" because they have no "imagination." What makes Kurtz remarkable is not only that he has lived in the darkness, but also chosen to leave it. It never leaves him, nor any man who has confronted it.

We are never told why Kurtz goes back with Marlow. On his trip back to civilization he dies with the words; "The horror! The horror!" Marlow visits Kurtz's intended in Brussels, a place he had described as a whitened sepulchre. She asks what his last words were. Marlow lies and tells her his last words were about her. As T.S. Eliot reminds us in the Four Quartets, human beings cannot bear too much reality.

When Kurtz dies on the steamer taking him down the Congo, his last words, "The horror! The horror!" impressive and even terrifying as they are, are nevertheless thoroughly ambiguous. They might represent Kurtz's final desire to return to the scene of those abominable satisfactions, be his judgement on the unworthiness of his end, a comment on the human condition, or a vision of eternal damnation. Marlow, however, is certain of his own interpretation; he sees Kurtz's last words as a confession, as a final attempt at self-purification: "a judgement upon the adventures of his soul upon this earth":

> This is the reason why I affirm that Kurtz was a remarkable man. He had something to say. He said it. Since I had peeped over the edge myself, I understand better the meaning of his stare, that could not see the flame of the candle, but was wide enough to embrace the whole universe, piercing enough to penetrate all the hearts that beat in the darkness. He had summed up - he had judged. "The horror!"

At the "heart of darkness," it seems, there is a piercing clarity - a vision of man's fate so unendurable that it can only remain nameless:

> He was a remarkable man. After all, this was the expression of some sort of belief; it had candour, it had conviction, it had a

vibrating note of revolt in its whisper, it had the appalling face of a glimpsed truth - the strange commingling of desire and hate. . . It is his extremity that I seem to have lived through. True, he had made that last stride, he had stepped over the edge, while I had been permitted to draw back my hesitating foot. And perhaps in this is the whole difference; perhaps all the wisdom, and all truth, and all sincerity; are just compressed into that inappreciable moment of time in which we step over the threshold of the invisible. Perhaps! I like to think my summing-up would not have been a word of careless contempt. Better his cry - much better. It was an affirmation, a moral victory paid for by innumerable defeats, by abominable terrors, by abominable satisfactions. But it was a victory! That is why I have remained loyal to Kurtz to the last.

Heart of Darkness ends with the suggestion that truth is unendurable in the context of everyday life, that what one needs in order to maintain an assurance of safety and comfort is some sustaining illusion to which one can be faithful. The story closes with the anonymous narrator - his voice recognizably muted and chastened - looking over the quiet reaches of the Thames, and assuring us that it, too, "seemed to lead into the heart of an immense darkness."

Apocalypse Now

The last book of the Bible is called the book of the Apocalypse - or the book of revelation. The first line of the book is: "A revelation of Jesus Christ, which God gave him so that he should tell his servants what is now to take place" (Apoc 1:1). This revelation is given to John the Seer. The Greek word for revelation is 'Apocalypsis' and it means the things that are hidden are now revealed. It also refers to a genre of literature that showed events on earth but at the same time showed that God was there. In the book of the Apocalypse we see events as they occur here - under the use of symbols of monsters and wars, yet in the end God, in Jesus, is triumphant.

Francis Ford Coppola used the term 'apocalypse' in his film "Apocalypse Now" (1979). The horrors of Vietnam take the place of the events in the book of the Apocalypse. It is a re-telling of Conrad's "Heart of Darkness", but now placed in the context of the war in Vietnam. Kurtz, the ivory trader gone native and mad in "Heart of Darkness" becomes Colonel Walter E. Kurtz who has also gone native and mad. He rules a little kingdom which is a microcosm of the way America tried to spread its influence in Indo-China in the 1960's. Kurtz in the film is played by Marlon Brando. Captain Benjamin L. Willard (Martin Sheen) is an army assassin sent to kill Kurtz. Willard is a functioning assassin, an incomplete human being. He is drawn by the figure of Kurtz and goes up river in Vietnam. His journey takes him through the Vietnam war zone, the gate of hell that leads to the heart of darkness.

The making of "Apocalypse Now" is a story in itself. Eleanor Coppola helped make a documentary, "Hearts of Darkness: A Filmmakers Apocalypse" which documents the trials and tribulations of those involved in the making of the film. Martin Sheen recounts his battle with alcoholism. Those who were involved experienced something of the heart of darkness.

I remember the build up to the release of "Apocalypse Now". There were many delays to the release of the film leading one critic to write "Apocalypse When?" Some critics said, wisely in their own view, that the film was over-hyped and over-budgeted. So when I went to see it in 1980 I wondered what to expect, in the end I wasn't expecting much.

The film begins with the voice of Jim Morrison of "The Doors" singing "The End". I sat bolt upright. I knew instinctively that I was in for a rough trip. I was right. Next is the sight of the helicopters over the jungle and the jungle is set in flames. "The End" contains the words:

'The killer awoke before Dawn, he put his boots on.
He took a face from the ancient gallery…
…and he came to a door…and he looked inside
Father, yes son, I want to kill you.'

This describes the end of the film where Willard comes face to face with Kurtz.
. . .
. . .
'This is the end'

At the end of the movie as Willard recuperates from imprisonment and gets over the death of one of his companions, he sits in Kurtz's temple compound. He knows Kurtz is waiting to kill him, where 'mind is excellent, but whose spirit is mad.' Kurtz reads from T. S. Eliot's "The Hollow Men" (as seen in the 2002 redux version)

'We are the hollow men
Leaning together
Headpiece filled with straw. Alas!
Our dried voices, when
We whisper together
Are quiet and meaningless
As wind in dry grass
Or rats' feet over broken glass
In our dry cellar
Shape without form, shade without colour
Paralysed force, gesture without motion;
Those who have crossed
With direct eyes to death's other Kingdom'

"The Hollow Men" enacts the despair of seeking truth but our attempts to make sense of reality and spirituality seem to end in despair. Personal experience is trapped in the immediate experience, the immediate accelerates and we are unable to see beyond them. The epigraph of Eliot's poem refers to the 'old guy', the stuffed effigy that is based on Guy Fawkes night. The hero of "The Heart of Darkness" and "Apocalypse Now", mistah Kurtz has an advantage over the hollow men, he is dead but they are only deadened. Kurtz and Guy Fawkes were but violent souls. The hollow men not in deaths' dream kingdom. The following lines of the poem describe Kurtz's world and Willard begins to see this in his inner world also:

'This is the dead land
This is the cactus land
Here the stone images
Are raised.'

Willard kills Kurtz and then leaves the compound and the jungle is in flames, we hear the words again "The horror! The horror!"

Yet in the face of the darkness and the strange images of the book of the Apocalypse, the book remains a book of hope. In the end all violence, death and evil are overcome. In chapter 19 the seer hears the songs of victory in heaven. He describes the new heavenly Jerusalem as the bride of the lamb, "His bride is ready and she has been able to dress herself in dazzling white linen, because her linen is made of the good deeds of the saints" (Apoc 19:8). Just as Jesus overcame the violence of his death with the resurrection, so those who suffer in love effect a transformation and their love and kind deeds make God present in the world and sow seeds for the time when all evil is overcome.

The new Heavens and the new Earth come from the old heaven and earth we dwell in. In the end the 'heart of darkness' is vanquished and replaced with the heart of love of God. The Heaven of the heavenly Jerusalem is described in the following lines:

> Then I saw a new heaven and a new earth; the first heaven and the first earth had disappeared now, and there was no longer any sea. I saw the holy city, the new Jerusalem, coming down out of heaven from God, prepared as a bride dressed for her husband. Then I heard a loud voice call from the throne, 'Look, here God lives among human beings. He will make his home among them; they will be his people, and he will be their God, God-with-them. He will wipe away all tears from their eyes, there will be no more death, and no more mourning or sadness or pain. The world of the past has gone.'

> Then the One sitting on the throne spoke. 'Look, I am making the whole of creation new. Write this, "What I am saying is trustworthy and will come true."' Then he said to me, 'It has already happened. I am the Alpha and the Omega, the Beginning and the End. I will give water from the well of life free to anybody who is thirsty; anyone who proves victorious will inherit these things; and I will be his God and he will be my son.
> (Apoc 21:1-7)

In the new Heaven there is no new temple, because God and the Lamb are themselves the temple (Apoc 21:22) and the radiant glory of God lights up the new Heaven.

Yet we live in the in-between times.

From Darkness to the Healing Light of Love

Jesus began the inauguration of this new kingdom by his death and resurrection, but the final victory to which the book of the Apocalypse points is in the future. We judge that which is immediate to us in the only unique reality. Pasolini had hoped to meet a Christ-like figure to help him face the darkness, but he did not meet one. His hope is the hope of many. Yet in the midst of our confusion some are called to be 'echoes of God's heart' and God is love (1 Jn 4:8, 1-6). John in his letter reminds us:

"Love consists in this:
it is not we who loved God,
but God loved us and sent his Son
to expiate our sins."   (1 Jn 4:10)

Etty Hillesum (1914-1943) was a young Dutch girl who, during the war, developed a strong spirituality in the face of the darkness of the War years. Her first name was Esther. Her parents were Jewish, but weren't practising Jews. Etty had no religious upbringing. Etty and her brothers, Mischa and Joop were intelligent and gifted. Etty left her father's school in 1932 and she took a Degree in Law at the University of Amsterdam. She then enrolled in the Faculty of Slavonic Languages and then she turned her mind to the study of psychology and it was during this time the Second World War broke out. Etty went for counselling to Julius Spier ('S' in her diaries). He was a "psychochirologist" - one who believed he could read peoples character traits from their hands. Etty became his assistant ('his Russian secretary') and even for a time his lover.

Spier introduced her to the world of prayer, spirituality and the figure of Jesus (she became very attached to the Gospel of Matthew, especially the Sermon on the Mount and the Beatitudes). Etty spoke of her inner torments and depression to Spier. She comments: "Paradoxical, though it may sound: S heals people by teaching them how to suffer and accept" (An Interrupted Life, p. 75). Here the life of Etty begins to throw light on Thérèse and enables us to appreciate Thérèse's journey to love. Thérèse, too, had to learn to suffer and accept. She would call this abandon. God's work with Etty (and by the same token Etty's work with God) throws light on how He works in the soul of Thérèse.

Etty describes her first journey into prayer. She describes how she was suddenly moved by an internal force to kneel and pray:

'*Sunday morning*. Last night, shortly before going to bed, I suddenly went down on my knees in the middle of this large room, between the steel chairs and the matting. Almost automatically. Forced to the ground by something stronger than myself. Some time ago, I said to myself, "I am a kneeler in training." I was still embarrassed by this act, as intimate as gestures of love that cannot be put into words either, except by a poet. A patient once said to S., "I sometimes have the feeling that God is right inside me, for instance when I hear the Saint Matthew Passion." And S., said something like, "At such moments you are completely at one with the creative and cosmic forces that are at work in every human being." And these creative forces are ultimately part of God, but you need courage to put that into words.

This phrase has been ringing in my ears for several weeks: you need courage to put that into words. The courage to speak God's name. S. once said to me that it took quite a long time before he dared to say "God" without feeling that there was something ridiculous about it.'

(Interrupted Life, p. 74)

Etty was coming to know that God is the ground of our being and is closer to us than we are to ourselves. Indeed, Etty came to love herself. She discovered there were many blocks and obstacles in her way to loving herself. She said:

'*26 August, Tuesday evening*. There is a really deep well inside me. And in it dwells God. Sometimes I am there, too. But more often stones and grit block the well, and God is buried beneath. Then He must be dug out again.

I imagine that there are people who pray with their eyes turned heavenward. They seek God outside themselves. And there are those who bow their heads and bury it in their hands. I think that these seek God inside.'

(Interrupted Life, p. 44)

She knew, by experience, of the dwelling of God within the soul of the person. By placing herself present to God and His love, she came to love herself and God and develop a universal compassion for all people. This was her healing.

In journeying with Thérèse, we hope to go on a similar journey to healing and love.

Etty realised how easy it was to be vindictive and to add to the store of anger and hate that had darkened the world. She shares many reflections on these themes. This is one I wish to share with you. She is reflecting on wars and disputes:

> 'All disasters stem from us. Why is there a war? Perhaps because now and then I might be inclined to snap at my neighbour. Because I and my neighbour and everyone else do not have enough love. Yet we could fight war and all its excrescences by releasing, each day, the love that is shackled inside us, and giving it a chance to live. And I believe that I will never be able to hate any human being for his so-called wickedness, that I shall only hate the evil that is within me, though hate is perhaps putting it too strongly even then. In any case, we cannot be lax enough in what we demand of others and strict enough in what we demand of ourselves.'
>
> (Interrupted Life, p. 95)

She always felt there was love shackled in her heart and now she was being called to release this love. Her way was the Way of the Cross. She had learned to forgive herself for the things she got wrong and now she saw her vocation as being a light of love in a place where God had been driven out. She was warned by her friends about the genocide of the Jews and they pleaded with her to allow them help her escape to London, but she said no. She said her job was to comfort God who was suffering in his people in the Camps. She refused to escape and, eventually, was brought to Westerbork, finally dying in Auschwitz in 1943. She spent her last days being a 'light in the darkness' for many who suffered in those places.

Etty felt that in spirit she was completely free. No hatred or malice could cover her now because of her deep love for all. She had no weapons to defeat the darkness, but she had love. Even if no-one else believed, she did and she used this weapon to help the vulnerable cope and find peace in their sufferings.

> 'It is not morbid individualism to work on oneself. True peace will come only when every individual finds peace within himself; when we have all vanquished and transformed our hatred for our

fellow human beings of whatever race - even into love one day, although perhaps that is asking too much. It is, however, the only solution. I am a happy person and I hold life dear indeed, in this year of Our Lord 1942, the umpteenth year of the war.'

(Interrupted Life, p. 145)

By being peace and love in herself, she helped to show a better way. It was the way of Gandhi and Martin Luther King. It was the way of Thérèse. It is the way of Jesus. They all point to a way we have not really tried. They all believed in beating evil with love, not by killing the person. This is the way of God.

I have never thought Thérèse's expression of being love in the heart of the church as being any way sentimental. I think it was very prophetic. In pointing to love, Thérèse is pointing to something that is often lacking. We speak of reforming structures and laws but few think of replacing the hard heart of unloving with the heart of love. St. Paul writes in 1 Cor 13 (a text beloved of Thérèse): "Though I command languages, both human and angelic - if I speak without love I am no more than a gong booming or a cymbal clashing." The way to healing our loneliness (a loneliness that is found in the heart of darkness) is to come to know God's love, come to love ourselves (the grace of all graces) and extend to others the fruits of this love in the Spirit. This is a journey I am on and Thérèse has been my guide in this journey of healing.

It is in this context that I see the vocation of Saint Thérèse of Lisieux as being an echo in our time of the very heart of God. She brings the light of Jesus to shine in our darkness and teaches us once again, in the words of the Gospel of John, that darkness does not overcome it (cf Jn 1:5). It is this heart of love that triumphs in God's time and makes all things new (Apoc 21:5).

The Holy Spirit is the fire of love at the heart of the church, yet so few allow him in. Thérèse was one. She shows us the way.

The Heart of Love

It is easier to portray the heart of darkness than the heart of love. Jesus came among us to reveal the love of God in his person. He told us to love one another as he loved us (Jn 13:34). The Holy Spirit was given to humanity so as to lead us to this love.

However God calls forth different saints to show us how to live. One such saint was Thérèse of Lisieux (1873-1897). She was a young Carmelite nun who lived quietly in Northern France in the Carmel of Lisieux. Through the Spirit, Jesus was the teacher of her heart. She meditated on sacred scripture. She longed to be many things - a warrior, a soldier, a priest and while she was seeking she meditated on chapter 13 of Paul's letter to the Corinthians.

Paul was writing to the Corinthians because of disputes and faction-fighting among different groups (("I belong to Paul", "I belong to Apostles", "I belong to Cephas", "I belong to Christ" (1 Cor 1:12)). Paul tells the Corinthians of Christ and him crucified. He is the heart of our belief. In chapters 12-14 he looks at the charismatic gifts of the community. These too cause dissention and jealousy. Paul tells them we are all parts of the body of Christ (1 Cor 12:12-13). Everyone has a part to play. Then he teaches them to meditate on the higher gifts. In chapter 13 we have his hymn to love; he tells us:

> Though I command languages both human and angelic - if I speak without love, I am no more than a gong booming or a cymbal clashing. And though I have the power of prophecy, to penetrate all mysteries and knowledge, and though I have all the faith necessary to move mountains - if I am without love, I am nothing. Though I should give away to the poor all that I possess, and even give up my body to be burned - if I am without love, it will do me no good whatever.

> Love is always patient and kind; love is never jealous; love is not boastful or conceited, it is never rude and never seeks its own advantage, it does not take offence or store up grievances. Love does not rejoice at wrongdoing, but finds its joy in the truth. It is always ready to make allowances, to trust, to hope and to endure whatever comes.

> Love never comes to an end. But if there are prophecies, they will be done away with; if tongues, they will fall silent; and if knowledge, it will be done away with. For we know only imperfectly; and we prophesy imperfectly; but when perfection comes, all imperfect things will be done away with.

> When I was a child, I used to talk like a child, and see things as a child does, and think like a child; but now that I have become an

adult, I have finished with all childish ways. Now we see only reflections in a mirror, mere riddles, but then we shall be seeing face to face. Now I can know only imperfectly; but then I shall know just as fully as I am myself known.

As it is, these remain: faith, hope and love, the three of them; and the greatest of them is love.

(1 Cor 13:1-13)

Paul knows that he himself does not fulfil all the words he uses - he is not always patient and kind. The Corinthians too know that they are not patient, kind and as the letter has let us know they are often jealous. The description of love is a description of Jesus. We are called to be like Jesus, by the working of the Holy Spirit.

Here is Thérèse's description of how she found her vocation, from her book "The Story of a Soul" Chapter 13 gave Thérèse a light, "Love is the most excellent way that leads to God." She had found her answer:

At last my mind was at rest . . . CHARITY gave me the key to my vocation. I understood that the Church had a body made up of different members, the most necessary and most noble of all could not be lacking, and so I understood that the Church had a heart, and that this heart was BURING WITH LOVE. I understood that it was LOVE ALONE that made the Church's members act, and that if love ever became extinct, apostles would not preach the Gospel, martyrs would refuse to shed their blood. I understood that LOVE CONTAINED ALL VOCATIONS, THAT LOVE WAS EVERYTHING, THAT IT EMBRACED ALL TIME AND ALL PLACES. IN A WORD, THAT IT IS ETERNAL!

Then, in the excess of my ecstatic joy, I cried out: O Jesus, my love, at last I have found my vocation. MY VOCATION IS LOVE!

Yes, I have found my place in the Church and it is you, O my God, who have given me this place - in the heart of the Church, my mother, I shall be LOVE. Thus I shall be everything - and thus my dream will be fulfilled!!!

(MsB, 3v°)

The Carmelite, after making this discovery which fulfilled all her desires, continues her dialogue with Jesus and changes the symbol. This universal vocation which she had found at last (she was nearly twenty-four), far from tearing her away from her everyday life would establish her in her hidden life. To do everything out of love would transform her completely. Little, weak, poor, like a small bird, asleep or distracted at prayer-time, still very imperfect, her strength would come from abandoning herself completely to love, from daring to believe with a reckless, bold abandon that her life offered to the divine sun (or divine eagle), Jesus, could save the world. By daring to believe, unconditionally, in this love, she would be an apostle, doctor, warrior, priest, martyr. Spectacular feats were denied her, but she could throw flowers, that is, offer up all the little occasions to love which life presented each day.

When we meditated on the heart of darkness we saw how real this heart was. In the prologue to John's Gospel we have this description of Jesus, the word made flesh.

"In the beginning was the Word,
the Word was with God
and the Word was God.
He was with God in the beginning.
Through him all things came into being
not one thing came into being
except through him.
What came into being in him was life,
that life was the light of man;
and light shines in the darkness
and darkness could not overpower it."   (Jn 1:2-5)

Jesus shows us that love ultimately wins out. He was crucified but was raised to life by God again. This showed that love is stronger than death.

Thérèse's offering of herself was something very real. In the last 18 months of her life she suffered in many ways. Her body was wracked by pain. Her faith was tested. God was silent - she shared Jesus' agony in Gethsemane and remained there with him in his lonely vigil. She described her trial of faith in the following words:

It seems that the darkness, borrowing the voice of sinners, says mockingly to me: 'You are dreaming about the light, about a country fragrant with the sweetest perfumes; you are dreaming about the eternal possession of the creator of all these marvels; you believe that one day you will walk out of this fog which surrounds you! Dream on, dream on; rejoice in death which will not give you what you hope for, but even deeper night, the night of nothingness.' (MsC, 6v°)

She describes herself as eating at the table of sinners.

Lord, your child has understood your divine light, and she begs your forgiveness for her brothers. She agrees to eat the bread of sorrow for as long as you wish, and she does not want to leave this table filled with bitterness where poor sinners are eating before the day you have appointed. But can she not also say in her own name and in the name of her brothers: 'Have pity on us, Lord, for we are poor sinners!' Oh! Lord, send us away justified. May all those who are not enlightened by the bright flame of faith see it shine one day: O Jesus! If the table defiled by them has to be purified by a soul who loves you, I will eat the bread of trial there alone until it please you to bring me into your luminous kingdom. (MsC, 6r°)

When, after her death "The Story of a Soul", her recollections were published, the book become a success. Those who read it saw in Thérèse a sister who was with them in their loneliness. Among the French soldiers in World War I, the book was one of their favourites. The hell of the trenches was where the soldiers came to appreciate the lonely prayer of Thérèse who prayed her darkness for people like them.

Pranzini:

Before Thérèse joined Carmel, she prayed for a convicted murderer called Pranzini. The year was 1887.

One Sunday in July, at the end of Mass a picture of Jesus crucified slipped from her missal. No one was collecting the blood he had shed. Thérèse decided that she would henceforth remain, in spirit, at the foot of that cross to collect that blood for sinners. Charity entered into my heart. She too would be a fisher of human beings. She thirsted like Jesus. Her vocation to Carmel became clear and deep. She felt the need to forget herself. The Pranzini affair provided her with the opportunity to put her desires into practice.

On the night of 19 to 20 March 1887 two women and a little girl were murdered, in a horrible way, at 17 Rue Montaingne in Paris. One, Régine de Montelle (her real name Marie Regnaud), was known in fashionable Parisian society for her fast living; the other was her maid. The child, who was twelve years old, undoubtedly belonged to the former. Jewellery had disappeared.

This triple crime aroused universal interest. Two days later the police arrested a suspect in Marseilles; he was Henri Pranzini, thirty years old and born in Alexandria. The charges mounted against this tall and handsome adventurer. He repeatedly denied them and did not seem to be a common criminal. Boldly he faced witnesses and judges. All the press in France and abroad followed the case from March to June and gave the most sordid details. The hearing began on 9 July and on the 13th Pranzini was condemned to death.

Thérèse heard about him. She had but one desire: to save his soul. When all the newspapers - including La Croix - were speaking only of 'the sinister scoundrel', 'the monster' or 'the vile brute', the young girl adopted him as her first child. For him, she prayed, she increased her sacrifices and asked Celine to have masses offered for him, without telling her of the intention! Her sister finally drew the secret from her and they united their efforts.

> I was convinced in the depths of my heart that our desires
> would be granted, but to give me courage to go on praying
> for sinners I told God I was sure he would pardon poor
> unfortunate Pranzini and that I would believe it even if he
> did not go to confession or show any sign of repentance. I
> had such confidence in Jesus' infinite mercy, but I was
> asking for a 'sign' of repentance, just for my own
> consolation. (MsA, 45v°-46r°)

On 31 August at dawn, in the Grande Roquette prison, Pranzini protested his innocence to the foot of the guillotine and refused the services of Abbé Faure, the chaplain. However at the last moment he called for the crucifix and kissed it twice before he died.

The next day, disregarding her father's ruling not to read the newspapers, Thérèse opened La Croix and read the account of Pranzini's death. She had to hide to conceal her tears. Her prayer had been heard to the letter! The sign she had asked for had been granted. It corresponded exactly to the grace Jesus had given her to draw her to pray for sinners: Pranzini had kissed the wounds of Jesus crucified whose blood Thérèse wanted to gather up for all the world.

This unique grace increased her determination to enter Carmel: to pray and to give her life for sinners. If the Lord had given her Pranzini as her first child, it was so that she would have a great many others.

In Martin Scorsese's film "Mean Streets" (1973) there is a parallel to Thérèse's prayer for Pranzini. Charlie (Harvey Keitel) is seen praying in a church but he believes the only way to overcome sin is 'on the streets,' to look after people there. Then we come to Tony (David Troval) and his bar. The bar and environment seem to be clothed in red. The effect is almost monochrome. Red is the colour of grace, Scorsese tries to show grace must work in the real world. Then in this surreal atmosphere Johnny Boy (Robert De Niro) walks in and Charlie says "Here comes my penance". All throughout the film he tries to look after Johnny Boy. Scorsese was trying to show grace but in these scenes he shows us how hard it is to love truly - especially when it comes to loving Johnny Boy. Love in reality is not the same as romantic ideas. It can be difficult and go without thanks. This was the love of Thérèse which was an echo of the heart of love of God revealed in Jesus.

St. Gregory of Nyssa (335 - 395) was one of the early Fathers of the Church. In his day, like ours, the heart of darkness, evil, seemed all-powerful. Yet he believed that in the end goodness would overcome evil, the heart of love would overcome the heart of darkness. Jesus showed by his resurrection that the darkness cannot overcome the light (Jn 1:5).

Chapter Two
Aspects of Love:

Édith Piaf (1915-1963) is known for her music and her delivery of a song. All her life was shrouded in mystery and tragedy. Simone Berteaut was a friend of Édith, Simone says that as a child she was blind from the age of 3 to 7. Her grandmother Louise took her to Lisieux and she could see again. Since then Édith had a devotion to Thérèse and kept a small picture of the saint always at her bedside table. Édith ('The little sparrow'- Piaf) was just one of the many troubled souls who found shelter in the loving prayer of Thérèse. This is beautifully seen in the 2007 film 'La Vie en Rose'. Édith is played by Marion Cotillard who gave an Oscar winning performance. She shows Edith's life to be made up of love, music, sorrow and tragedy.

Many reported cures, physical and psychological, have been attributed to the intercession of Thérèse. She had written in one of her final letters to Pére Roulland that she intended to continue working in heaven for the love of all (LT 254).

The Suffering of Love:

Thérèse, as we will see, often spoke about suffering. Many find this part difficult, yet it is necessary to see the context in which she sees suffering. It is in the context of her vocation to be 'love' in the heart of the church (MsB, 3v°). Love involves sacrifice and suffering on behalf of the beloved. Thérèse loved God and shared Jesus' agony as he was rejected, yet continued to love to bring healing to a fallen world, the world that had come to have a heart of darkness. The example of the suffering of love that often comes to my mind is the example of a young couple whose child is taken ill and rushed to hospital. I have met many such couples and as they wait in the corridors for news. Their suffering is very real. As they sit by the bed of their child their anxiety and suffering is real. This is only so because of the love that is in their hearts - if they did not love and care, they would not suffer.

It is something the same as the 'mystical nights' that the saints like Thérèse undergo. It is a sharing in Jesus' mission of love. Because Jesus loves all, he wills to share and take to himself the experience of sin, loneliness and alienation of all. He secretly enters each person's solitariness and isolation and they become his. Thérèse is called to love and be with Jesus in this lonely passion which continues throughout time. She gave herself away to Jesus and surrendered herself to be with him in his lonely passion for the benefit of a new creation that is not yet revealed, but where every tear will be wiped away.

Herbert McCabe, O.P., in his book, God Matters (1987), wrote the following insightful piece:

> "The mission of Jesus from the Father is not the mission to be crucified; what the Father wished is that Jesus should be human .
> . . . And this is what Jesus sees as a command laid on him by his Father in heaven; the obedience of Jesus to his Father is to be totally, completely human. This is his obedience, an expression of his love for the Father; the fact that to be human means to be crucified is not something that the Father has directly planned but what we have arranged. We have made a world in which there is no way of being human that does not involve suffering."
>
> (God Matters, p.93)

We learn we are young that the world can be a cruel and heartless place where the good suffer. Speculation about why this is so, is often excessively reductionistic, making what isn't all right seem okay. Yet stories like 'The Heart of Darkness', 'Apocalypse Now' and 'Mean Streets' lay bare the evil that lurks in the world better than any philosophical speculation. Martin Scorsese had tried to show grace at work in 'Mean Streets'. Yet in films such as 'Taxi Driver' (1976), 'Raging Bull' (1980), 'Goodfellas' (1990) and 'Gangs of New York' (2002) he was able to portray hell and violence better than his attempt at showing grace. These films were also more successful.

We have made a world in which there is no way of being human and loving that does not involve suffering. Jesus came as a vulnerable, loving human being who gave love unconditionally to all who come to him for healing. In the prologue of the Gospel of John we are told:

> "He was in the world
> that had come into being through him,
> and the world did not recognise him.
> He came to his own
> and his own people did not accept him." (Jn 1:10-11)

We are his own people. Jesus was brought to the cross and death by the rejection of a loveless world. Yet he was raised to life by God and he offered new life, pardon and reconciliation to all who would receive him. Love was stronger than hate, the heart of darkness and death. Yet the final victory that we see in figurative form in the Book of the Apocalypse awaits in future time when Jesus' victory will be complete.

We live in the in-between time and Jesus calls others to join him in his works of healing the world. We see this in his call of the apostle Paul. In the letter to the Galatians Paul says: "I have been crucified with Christ, and yet I am alive; yet it is no longer I but Christ living in me. The life I am now living, subject to the limitations of human nature, I am living in faith, faith is the son of God who loved me and gave himself for me." (Gal 1:19-21). Paul has come to know he is loved by God and now becomes one with Jesus to co-operate with him in his work of reconciliation and healing. In the words of the letter to the Colossians, "It makes me happy to suffer for you now and in my own body to make up all the hardship that still has to be undergone by Christ for the sake of his body, the Church . . . (Col 1:24) In the second letter to the Corinthians Paul describes his sufferings and the life they produce in his flock:

"But we hold this treasure in pots of earthenware, so that the immensity of the power is God's and not our own. We are subjected to every kind of hardship, but never distressed; we see no way out but we never despair; we are pursued but never cut off; knocked down, but still have some life in us; always we carry with us in our body the death of Jesus so that the life of Jesus, too, may be visible in our body. Indeed, while we are still alive, we are continually being handed over to death, for the sake of Jesus, so that the life of Jesus, too, may be visible in our mortal flesh. In us, then, death is at work; in you, life." (2 Cor 4:6-12)

Paul here suffers his weaknesses yet God acts through our weaknesses (see 2 Cor 12:8-10). Paul suffers in union with Jesus. Yet God was all the time working through his weaknesses bringing life to Paul's comments. In union with Christ suffering has been given a meaning and from suffering with Jesus, wounds are healed. The sufferings of love heal the wounds of unloving. Paul often uses the term 'in Christ' to show his union by the love of the Holy Spirit with Jesus. In 1 Peter 2:24 we have the succinct phrase 'by his wounds you have been healed'. Thérèse and the other saints are called to share in Jesus' work for our healing and salvation (the Greek word 'sozein' means both to heal and save). Paul summed up his life in Christ in the letter to the Philippians:

"But what were once my assets I now through Christ Jesus count as losses. Yes, I will go further: because of the supreme advantage of knowing Christ Jesus my Lord, I count everything else as loss. For him I have accepted the loss of all other things, and look on them all as filth if only I can gain Christ and be given a place in him, with the uprightness I have gained not from the Law, but through faith in Christ, an uprightness from God, based on faith, that I may come to know him and the power of his resurrection, and partake of his sufferings by being moulded to the pattern of his death, striving towards the goal of resurrection from the dead.
(Phil 3:7-11)

He has come to know Jesus and the power of his resurrection. He is in love with the risen Jesus and the love of Jesus has been passed into his heart by the Holy Spirit (Rom 5:5).

He urges his congregation in the faith of confidence and love.

"Always be joyful, then, in the Lord; I repeat, be joyful. Let your good sense be obvious to everybody. The Lord is near. Never worry about anything; but tell God all your desires of every kind in prayer and petition shot through with gratitude, and the peace of God which is beyond our understanding will guard your hearts and your thoughts in Christ Jesus. Finally, brothers, let your minds be filled with everything that is honourable, everything that is upright and pure, everything that we love and admire - with whatever is good and praiseworthy. Keep doing everything you learnt from me and were told by me and heard or seen me doing. Then the God of peace will be with you."
(Phil 4:4-9)

As we come to know God revealed by Jesus we can entrust ourselves as we are to the tender mercy of God. We remain faithful to this grace by our very way of acting. These readings show us how close Thérèse was to the spirit of the sacred writings.

Snapshots of Thérèse

To give a complete biography of Thérèse is a monumental work in itself. Guy Gaucher's 2010 biography of Thérèse, to which I am deeply indebted, is over 600 pages long. What I intend to do on our journey to understand the little way is to give some snapshots of Thérèse, a sort of impressionistic picture of her life.

Thérèse's life was under the guidance of the Holy Spirit. St. Paul tells us in his letter to the Romans: "We are well aware that God works with those who love him, those who have been called in accordance with his purpose, and turn everything to their good" (Rom 8:28). Thérèse knew the experience of loss, illness and loneliness. She admitted that she had never known a day without suffering in her life in the Carmel in Lisieux (Last Conversation, p.268). Yet she loved God and surrendered all these sufferings into his hands to ease others pain - she saw everybody's pain in the pain of Jesus. She spoke regularly of consoling Jesus (e.g., LT 96). She lived out the words of St. Paul who also said in Romans, "if we have been joined to him by dying, so shall we share a resurrection like his" (Rom 6:5). By suffering he helped to help others reach peace with God and the fullness of healing to be found in him.

(a) Early Childhood:

Psychology has revealed the importance of the beginnings of each life. Thérèse's parents, Zélie and Louis Martin were very loving, holy and devout. In fact in 2008 in Lisieux Pope Benedict XVI beatified them. This is one of the steps towards sainthood.

Thérèse's early days were 'sunny years'. She tells us how "everything smiled upon me on this earth. I found flowers under each of my steps and my happy disposition also contributed to making my life pleasant" (MsA, 11v° and 12r°). Thérèse tells us how special her parents were. She received "smiles and most tender caresses". Thérèse's parents were loving and sensitive. Zélie said that Thérèse was very intelligent and remembered everything. She could however be very nervous, very sensitive and brought easily to tears and could be obstinate and throw tantrums. She could be very stubborn. Thérèse spoke of her experience of being loved in a letter she wrote in 1896. She said, "Our Lord wanting my first glance for himself alone, saw first to ask for my heart from the cradle, if I can so express myself" (LT 201). Her parents taught her to always have confidence in God and give oneself to him in total abandonment. One of Thérèse's first desires as a child was to hide herself beneath the shadow of the virginal mantle of the mother of God (MsA, 57r°).

However at the age of four Thérèse lost her mother. Zélie had been very ill for several years. Even at the time of Thérèse's birth she had been ravaged by bone cancer and this had caused her intense pain. This reveals her heroism. Deprived of the affection of an incomparable mother (MsA, 4v°) Thérèse felt an acute wound in her heart. "After Mama's death" she admits "my happy disposition changed completely; I, once so full of life and so open, became timid and retiring, sensitive to the extreme. One glance was enough to reduce me to tears and I was happy only when left completely alone. I couldn't bear the company of strangers and found my joy only within the intimacy of my family" (MsA, 13r°).

Elsewhere she describes at that time to be 'timid and sensitive' (MsA, 22v°), 'sweet but much given to crying' (MsA, 24r°) yet for her family, Louis, and sisters Léonie, Pauline, Marie and her little Céline loved her and sustained her.

(b) The loss of a second Mother:

Pauline became the surrogate mother of Thérèse, but one day during the summer of 1882 Thérèse overheard Pauline and Marie talking. She came to hear that she was going to lose Pauline who was going to join the Carmel in Lisieux.

> It was like a sword piercing my heart. I did not know what Carmel was, but I understood that Pauline was going to leave me and enter a convent. I understood that she WOULD NOT WAIT FOR ME and that I was going to lose my second mother! Ah! How can I express the anguish in my heart. In an instant I understood what life was; until then I had not imagined it could be so sad, but it appeared to me in its stark reality. I saw that it was only continual suffering and separation. I shed very bitter tears.   (MsA, 26r°)

Pauline, in the first fervour of her vocation, did not realise she had deeply hurt her sister. Very much later she would bitterly regret her behaviour 'Ah! If I had known it would cause her to suffer so much, I would have gone about it in another way. I would have told her everything!'

Thérèse's health deteriorated and she began to suffer from continual headaches and pains in her side and stomach. She had never been happy in school. She was lonely and sensitive and could not stand up for herself. She became even more ill and was confined to bed. Her family were concerned about her; fearing that they were going to lose their little angel. Louis had brought a statue of Our Lady to look after the tormented little one. Thérèse recounts the following story:

> Finding no help on earth, poor little Thérèse also turned towards her heavenly Mother and prayed with all her heart for her to have pity on her at last. All of a sudden the blessed Virgin appeared to me beautiful, more beautiful than anything I had ever seen before. Her face expressed an ineffable goodness and tenderness, but what went right to the depths of my soul was THE BLESSED VIRGIN'S RAVISHING SMILE. Then all my pain vanished, two large tears welled up on my eyelashes and silently rolled down my cheeks, but they were tears of pure joy. Ah! I thought, the blessed Virgin has smiled at me, how happy I am - but I will never tell anyone, for then MY HAPPINESS WOULD DISAPPEAR.
>
> (MsA, 30r°-v°)

The three sisters witnessed this scene and the relaxed condition of the sick child. The next day she resumed her ordinary life. During the following months, in the garden, Leonie found her there in distress. She fell down and remained stretched out for some moments, her body rigid. But there was no delirium or violent spasm. From that time there was no recurrence of any trouble of this kind.

But Thérèse remained psychologically delicate, and those around her were deeply affected by that dramatic illness. The doctor warned the family to avoid any violent emotion which could be harmful to the child, and each did their best to coddle her more.

(c) Anxiety and Scruples:

In one of her retreats in May 1885 Thérèse heard the Abbé tell the children about mortal sin. This was too much for Thérèse. She saw the possibility of offending God at every turn. She was sure she merited hell. I remember as a young adolescent we had a very poor religious textbook and it made all of us very scrupulous and heaven seemed like a place very few might reach. Thérèse said one 'would have to endure this martyrdom to understand what it was like.

It would be impossible for me to say what I suffered for eighteen months' (MsA, 39r°). Marie, who had taken over as mother from Pauline, coached Thérèse on how to go to confession, so her confessor didn't realise the anxiety state their little penitent was in.

To whom could she now confide the scruples which obsessed her? She made difficulties out of everything. Her spiritual crisis came to a head. Was she going to have a relapse? Once again she obeyed an instinctive reflex: not finding anyone on earth, she turned to heaven. In her loneliness Thérèse suddenly remembered her little brothers and sisters who had died before she was born.

> I spoke to them with the simplicity of a child, pointing out that, as the youngest in the family, I had always been the most loved, the one who had been showered with my sisters' tender care. Their going to heaven did not seem to me to be a reason for forgetting me; on the contrary, finding themselves in a position to draw from the divine treasures, they had to get PEACE for me and thereby show me that, in heaven, they still knew how to love. (MsA, 44r°)

From the pit of her distress this was Thérèse's spontaneous prayer. The answer was not long in coming, for soon peace poured into my soul and I knew that I was as loved in heaven as I was on earth. Since then, my devotion to my little brothers and sisters has increased.

She never forgot that healing experience. All of a sudden her scruples disappeared; but her over-sensitiveness remained.

The story of her full overcoming of the anxiety of scruples did continue in many ways however. When she was a nun in Carmel she was assured by Father Pichon, spiritual advisor to the Martin sisters but now resident in that Thérèse had never (he emphasised never) committed a mortal sin. This gave Thérèse further healing.

In a retreat given by a Franciscan Father Prou from 7 to 15 October 1891 Thérèse was launched on a new path. Father Prou was a stand-in and was more accustomed to talking to workers and dockers. The Carmelite sisters did not think he would have much to help them as he was more accustomed to hardened sinners! However there was one who really appreciated Fr. Prou - our little Thérèse. He launched her on the way to sainthood.

Fr. Prou's zealous preaching on abandonment and mercy expanded her heart. Even more so his spiritual direction. She who normally had so much trouble speaking about her inner life, after a few words to the Franciscan felt herself

> Understood in a marvellous way. My soul was like a book which the priest read better than I did. He launched me full sail on the waves of confidence and love which held such an attraction for me, but upon which I had not dared to venture. He told me that my faults did not offend God, and, taking God's place as he did, he told me in his name that God was very pleased with me.
>
> (MsA, 80v°)

This brought her great light and joy! She had never heard that faults could not offend God. As for confidence and love, they attracted her so much! But in the climate which surrounded her, she had not dared to go that way.

She was launched on the waves of confidence and love.

(d) Her Conversion (1886) (MsA, 45r°)

Céline described her sister as a baby. There was a custom of putting presents into stockings in front of the fireplace at Christmas. At fourteen Thérèse still wanted to do it.

> While she was going up the narrow stairs she heard her father, who was tired, say to Céline: 'Well, fortunately this will be the last year!' Seeing Thérèse's tears, her sister realised that the midnight supper was spoilt. She advised her not to go back downstairs immediately. But it was then that everything suddenly changed. In an instant Thérèse recovered herself, dried her eyes, went down and, full of joy, opened the parcels. Céline could not believe it!
>
> On the stairs a complete transformation had taken place in her sister. A new unknown strength suddenly came upon her. She was no longer the same. Jesus had changed her heart. The night in which she had been living was changed into brilliant light. The account which we have of this conversion is dated 1895. Nine years later Sister Thérèse of The Child Jesus could judge the permanence of her sudden transformation. For she could not doubt: it was a little miracle. In an instant Jesus, content with my

good will, accomplished the work I had not been able to do in ten years. On that 25 December 1886 Thérèse passed a major milestone in her life which marked the beginning of the third period of her existence, the most beautiful of all. After nine sad years (1881-6 in particular) she had recovered the strength of soul she had lost when her mother died and, she said, she was to retain it forever.

An admirable exchange had just taken place between the Infant in the manger who had taken upon himself frail human nature, and little Thérèse, who had become strong. It was a Eucharistic grace: I had the happiness, on that night, of receiving the strong and powerful God.

Suddenly she was freed from the faults and imperfections of childhood. This grace made her grow up and mature. Her tears dried up. Her over-sensitiveness was cured. At last she was equipped to live. Since that blessed night, I have not been vanquished in any battle, but on the contrary, I have marched from victory to victory and begun, so to speak, 'TO RUN A GIANT'S COURSE' (Ps. 19:5)

That night another Thérèse Martin was born. Jesus changed me in such a way that I no longer knew myself. Or rather, he had just returned her to herself, out of a bad dream which had lasted for years, the most dramatic moments of which had been her strange illness and her crisis of scruples. It was not her real nature to be weepy, dreamy and weak-willed. In Alençon she had not been like that. After the smile of the Blessed Virgin, the intercession of her little brothers and sisters, the Infant of Christmas - the strong God - had at last set her free. Thérèse became herself. It was a decisive fundamental happening. Henceforth she was to know, forever, that God had saved her, Thérèse from shipwreck. It was an irreversible experience. Now she was armed for war!

(see G. Gaucher, Story of a Life, p.197f)

(e) Face to Face:

There are so many other things that could be written about Thérèse and still not enough would be said. I content myself for the moment with the above snapshots. During all this time of trial Thérèse drew closer to the figure of Jesus. At her first communion she felt a profound joy in receiving the blessed sacrament (MsA, 36v°). She describes it as the sacrament of love. Later as a Carmelite in 1895 when Thérèse was making the stations of the Cross she felt she was seized with 'so violent a love of God' that she believed she was immersed in love. "I was burning with love" (see Descouvement, Thérèse, p240). She was one in union of love with Jesus by the fire of the Holy Spirit.

In April 1889, Thérèse wrote to Céline. She told her 'Jesus is on fire with love for us . . . Look at his adorable face! . . .Look at his eyes lifeless and lowered! Look at his wounds . . .Look at Jesus in His Face . . . Here you will see how He loves us' (LT87). At this time Louis had become ill, but gave himself (to use Thérèse's term abandoned) himself to suffering. Thérèse saw his sufferings as a share in Christ's humiliation. This adds more poignancy to Thérèse's words.

Mother Geneviève, the foundress of the Carmel in Lisieux advised the novice to have a devotion to the Holy Face of the crucified one. The idea of face is something I found in the philosophy of Emmanuel Levinas (1906-1995). He was a Lithuanian born French Jewish philosopher and Talmudic commentator. Levinas preferred to think of philosophy as the 'wisdom of love' rather than the love of wisdom (the literal Greek meaning of the word 'philosophy'). In his view responsibility precedes any objective searching after birth. In his work "Totality and Infinity", the encounter 'face to face' with another is a privileged phenomenon in which the other person's proximity and distance are both firmly felt. "The Other precisely reveals himself in his alterity not in a shock negating the I, but as the primordial phenomenon of gentleness" (Totality and Infinity, p.150). One recognises the transcendence of the other. What Levinas says applies in a special way to Thérèse and her contemplation of the love revealed in Jesus. From her truth had been accustomed to venerating the Holy face of Jesus, as it was represented in what was thought to be Veronica's veil preserved in St. Peter and a reproduction of which had been placed in Saint-Pierre Cathedral in Lisieux. Just as the face of Zélie and Louis gave her life, so now the contemplation of the Holy Face led her to a new life in the Spirit. Thérèse often reflected on the sacred face in the light of Is 53. The relation to the Holy Face of Jesus helped lead to the union of love that was forged between Thérèse and Jesus by the Holy Spirit. She added the name 'Saint-Face' to her religious name. She called herself 'Thérèse de L'Enfant Jesus et de la Sainte Face' (Thérèse of The Infant Jesus and The Holy Face).

Chapter Three
Looking Unto Jesus (Heb 12:2)

To begin to understand Thérèse's doctrine we must look at the world she inherited. For centuries France and most of the Catholic world was influenced by a movement called Jansenism. This was a movement begun by the Dutch theologian Cornelius Jansen (+1638) and popularised by Jansen's friend, Jean de Vargier (+1643). It was based on a rigid interpretation of Augustine. It emphasised original sin, human depravity, the necessity of divine grace and predestination. Pope Innocent X in 1653, in the bull 'Cum Occasione' condemned Jansenism as a movement.

Among those influenced by Jansenism was Blaise Pascal (+1662). To show the extremes of Jansenism one only has to look at the final days of Pascal. When he was dying he was refused Holy Communion because the Jansenists did not think he was worthy. Their judgements were harsh and the idea that we were all far from God dominated their world.

Pascal had a poor man brought to him - he said the poor man was the sacrament of the poor Christ. The negative view of Jansenism, its emphasis on human depravity and fear of the judgment of God were strong influences for centuries. Indeed I can now see how Jansenism influenced some of my earlier teachers in the faith. It was for them a faith based on fear, damnation and the harsh judgment of God. This helps us understand the emphasis on judgment and becomes 'victim of God's justice' was so prevalent in Thérèse's time.

Thérèse was influenced by the negative views of Jansenism. The influence of Jansenism and its emphasis on sin, depravity, hell and the loss of God was still widespread. Abbé Louis-Victor Domin (1843-1918) who was chaplain to the Benedictines in Lisieux was confessor and catechist to Thérèse as she prepared for her first confession and communion. He was influenced by Jansenism and its harshness. He preached two retreats to prepare the young Thérèse for her first holy communion. Thérèse took notes on his conferences from the 5th to 7th May 1884. She notes how Abbé Domin preached to them on the tortures of Hell and it depended on how one approached one's first holy communion whether one would go to Heaven or experience all those tortures. She also tells of the conference the Abbé gave on sacrilegious communion and said things that terrified Thérèse (see Clapier, Amier jusqu'à mourir d'amour, p.43).

In a second retreat given from 17th to 20th May 1895 when Thérèse was getting ready for her second communion Abbé Domin's emphasis on hell and loss gave Thérèse scruples, a sickness she would suffer from for at least eighteen months until she prayed to her deceased brothers and sisters to pray for her (MsA, 44r°) and she found relief in their prayers. In her notes for this retreat Thérèse tells us that in his conferences Abbé Domin emphasised mortal sin and how if one fell into it then we could never reach God (Clapier, p.44). The emphasis was totally on judgement. Mercy and forgiveness were not emphasised. Thérèse tells us in MsA, 39r° that these thoughts provoked great anxiety in her and she had to pass through "terrible sickness of scruples". This anxiety would haunt Thérèse for quite a long time. As time wore on Thérèse came to know Jesus in her heart and he would become the interior teacher of her soul. He revealed to her the tenderness of the heart of God. So Thérèse became a counter-sign to the severity of the early teachings she had received.

The author of the letter to the Hebrews says: "Let us keep our eyes fixed on Jesus, who leads us in our faith and brings it to perfection; for the sake of the joy which lay ahead of him he endured the cross, disregarding the shame of it and has taken his seat at the right hand of God's throne" (Heb 12:2). Thérèse, in that explicitly, mentioning this text lived it to the full and she can be said to be a true spiritual theologian.

Thérèse's Experiences

In 1895 Thérèse's sister Pauline (now Mother Agnes of Jesus) asked her to write an account of her experiences. This became known as Manuscript A (MsA) and formed part of what we now know as "The Story of a Soul". She begins in the following way:

> Before taking up my pen, I knelt before the statue of Mary (the one that has given so many proofs of the maternal preferences of heaven's Queen for our family), and I begged her to guide my hand that it trace no line displeasing to her. Then opening the Holy Gospels my eyes fell on these words: 'And going up a mountain, he called to him men of his own choosing, and they came to him' (Mk. 3:13). This is the mystery of my vocation, my whole life, and especially the mystery of the privileges Jesus showered on my soul. He does not call those who are worthy but those whom He pleases or as St. Paul says: God will have mercy

on who, he will have mercy, and he will show pity to whom he will show pity. So then there is question not of him who wills nor of him who runs, but of God showing mercy" (Rom. 9:15-16).

Her manuscript becomes a testimony to God's mercy and love in her life.

She records in MsA (47v° -48r°) her sharing with Céline in moments of prayer:

Jesus, wanting to have us advance together, formed bonds in our hearts stronger than blood. He made us become spiritual sisters, and in us were realized the words of St. John of the Cross' Canticle (speaking to her spouse, the bride exclaims):

Following Your footprints
Maidens run lightly along the way;
The touch of (48r°) a spark,
The special wine,
Cause flowings in them from the balsam of God.

Yes, it was very lightly that we followed in Jesus' footprints. The sparks of love He sowed so generously in our souls, and the delicious and strong wine He gave us to drink made all passing things disappear before our eyes, and from our lips came aspirations of love inspired only by Him. How sweet were the conversations we held each evening in the belvédère! With enraptured gaze we beheld the white moon rising quietly behind the tall trees, the silvery rays it was casting upon the sleeping nature, the bright stars twinkling in the deep skies, the light breath of the evening breeze making the snowy clouds float easily along; all this raised our souls to heaven, that beautiful heaven whose "obverse side" alone we were able to contemplate.

Later on after both had become Carmelite nuns, Thérèse made her oblation to merciful love, Mother Agnes asked her to repeat her experience often during the day. Thérèse told her the following: This is the text from the work 'Last Conversations' (DE).

I asked her to explain what happened when she made her Act of Oblation to Merciful Love. First she said:

"Little Mother, I told you this when it took place,
but you paid no attention to me."

This was true; I'd given her the impression that I placed no importance on what she was saying.

"Well I was beginning the Way of the Cross; suddenly I was seized with such a violent love for God that I can't explain it except by saying it felt as though I were totally plunged into fire. Oh! What fire and what sweetness at one and the same time! I was on fire with love, and I felt that one minute more, one second more, and I wouldn't be able to sustain this ardour without dying. I understood, then, what the saints were saying about these states which they experienced so often. As for me, I experienced it only once and for one single instant, falling back immediately into my habitual state of dryness."

And later on:

"At the age of fourteen, I also experienced transports of love. Ah! How I loved God! But it wasn't at all as it was after my Oblation to Love; it wasn't a real flame that was burning in me." (DE, 7.7.2)

In the same month Mother Agnes pressed Thérèse and she confided to Agnes how she had experienced what a 'flight of the spirit was'. This was something Teresa of Avila had described in her "The Interior Castle" (6:5). This is where one feels the presence of God by his empowering presence, the Holy Spirit and one feels a sense of joy and peace. Thérèse says:

During Matins, She spoke to me about her prayers of former days, in the summer evenings during the periods of silence; and she understood then by experience what a "flight of the spirit" was. She spoke to me about another grace of this kind which she received in the grotto of St. Mary Magdalene, in the month of July, 1889, a grace followed by several days of "quietude."

"... It was as though a veil had been cast over all the things of this earth for me. . . . I was entirely hidden under the Blessed Virgin's veil. At this time, I was placed in charge of the refectory, and I could recall doing things as though not doing them; it was as if someone had lent me a body, I remained that way for one whole week." (DE, 11.7.2)

Her sisters were telling her that souls who reached perfect love like her, saw their beauty and she was among their number. Thérèse said she didn't see any beauty at all. All she could see were the graces she received from God (DE 10.8.2).

The presence of God was real for Thérèse. He was equally present in darkness and suffering. He was at work there as much as he was in the moments of light. She said she realised that Jesus lived in her, teaching, guiding and inspiring her (MsA, 83v°). She has also become aware that God is aware of our fragile nature. She asks: "What should I fear then? Ah! Must not the infinitely just God who deigns to pardon the faults of the prodigal son with as much kindness be just toward me who am with him always" (MsA 83v°-84r°). All her life became transparent to the workings of God in her soul. In manuscript C (MsC) written for Mother Marie de Gonzague, who was prioress in Thérèse's last years, Thérèse says:

> Your Love has gone before me, and it has grown with me, and now it is an abyss whose depths I cannot fathom. Love attracts love, and, my Jesus, my love leaps towards Yours; it would like to fill the abyss which attracts it, but alas! It is not even like a drop of dew lost in the ocean! For me to love You as You love me, I would have to borrow Your own Love, and then only would I be at rest. O my Jesus, it is perhaps an illusion but it seems to me that You cannot fill a soul with more love than the love with which You have filled mine; it is for this reason that I dare to ask You "to love those whom you have given me with the love with which you loved me." One day, in heaven if I discover You love them more than me, I shall rejoice at this, recognizing that these souls merit Your Love much more than I do; but here on earth, I cannot conceive a greater immensity of love than the one which it has pleased You to give me freely, without any merit of my part.
>
> (MsC, 35r°)

Thérèse came to see at an early age that loving and caring for salvation and healing means suffering with Jesus. At her confirmation she had the following experience, she felt the gentle presence of the Holy Spirit like Elijah felt on Mount Horeb (1 Kings 19:12-13) and she received the strength to bear the sufferings of love (MsA, 36v°-37r°). When she made her vows she experienced an influx of peace. She again mentions the gentle breeze of Elijah which signifies the presence of God in the Holy Spirit. (MsA 76v°). This was how she learned to suffer with love and live and die for love and to make God's love known to all, especially those who seemed far away. His love is boundless and Thérèse was a great teacher of this. This love is not loved. Many are blinded to it - Thérèse gave herself to heal this blindness and allow perfect love cast out fear. (1 Jn 4:18).

I of Thérèse - Thou of Jesus

Personalist philosophies and psychologies show us the importance of the other for the development of the person. The parents have a special place in our early formation. Thérèse had the love of Zélie and Louis. Later she had the love of her sisters. Martin Buber (+1965) spoke of the value of the "I - thou" relationship.

According to Buber the need for relationship is innate. The child has a drive for contact. "Man" Buber stated does not exist as a separate entity; "Man is a creation of the between" (I and Thou, p. 54). There are basically two types of in-between's which Buber characterised as 'I-Thou' and 'I-It'. The 'I-It' is a relationship between a person and equipment, a functional relationship, a relationship wholly lacking mutability.

The 'I-Thou' relationship is a wholly mutual relationship involving a full experiencing of the other. "Relation is reciprocity" (I and Thou, p.58). Not only is the 'Thou' relationship different from the 'It' but the 'I' is different. My 'I' is formed differently in the two relationships. When one relates to an 'It' one holds back something of oneself. When one relates to a 'Thou' one's whole being is involved. Nothing can be withheld

> "The basic word I-You can only be spoken along with one's whole being. The concentration and fusion into a whole being can never be accomplished by me, can never be accomplished without me. I require a Thou to become: becoming I, I say Thou. . ."
>
> (I and Thou, p. 62)

If one relates to another with less than one's being, if one holds something back, relating through greed or anticipation of some return, or if one remains in an objective attitude as a kind of spectator then one has moved from the 'I-Thou' to 'I-It'

To relate to another is a need-less fashion, one must lose or transcend oneself. Buber gave an illustration of the 'I-Thou' relationship from an incident in his youth. He used to look after a horse on his grandparents' estate:

> When I was eleven years of age, spending the summer on my grandparents' estate, I used, as often as I could do it unobserved, to steal into the stable and gently stroke the neck of my darling, a broad dapple-gray horse. It was not a casual delight but a great, certainly friendly, but also deeply stirring happening. If I am to explain it now, beginning from the still very fresh memory of my hand, I must say that what I experienced in touch with the animal was the Other, the immense otherness of the Other, which, however, did not remain strange like the otherness of the ox and the ram, but rather let me draw near and touch it. When I stroked the mighty mane, sometimes marvellously smooth-combed, at other times just as astonish wild, and felt the life beneath my hand, it was as though the element of vitality itself bordered on my skin, something that was not I, was certainly not akin to me, palpably the other, not just another, really the Other itself; and yet it let me approach, confided itself to me, placed itself elementally in the relation of Thou and Thou with me. The horse, even when I had not begun by pouring oats for him into the manger, very gently raised his massive head, ears flicking, then snorted quietly, as a conspirator; and I was approved. But one time - I do not know what came over the child, at any rate it was childlike enough - it struck me about the stroking, what fun it gave me, and suddenly I became conscious of my hand. The game went on as before, but something had changed, it was no longer the same thing. And the next day, after giving him a rich feed, when I stroked my friend's head he did not raise his head.
>
> (Buber, Between Man and Man, p.22f).

The basic experiential mode of the I-Thou is "dialogue," in which, either silently or spoken, "each of the participants has in mind the other or others in their particular being and turns to them with the intention of establishing a living mutual relation between himself and them." Dialogue is simply the turning toward another with one's whole being. When the young Buber turned away from the horse, became aware of his hand, and of how much pleasure the stroking afforded him, then dialogue vanished, and "monologue" and the I-It reigned. Buber termed this turning away from the other "reflexion." In reflexion not only is one "concerned with himself," but, even more important, one forgets about the particular being of the other.

Viktor Frankl, too, in his psychotherapy emphasised the healing power of "encounter" and criticised the vulgarisation of the term. In 1965 Pope Paul VI said in Ecclesiam Suam that the hope of the Second Vatican Council was that the Church would be a church of dialogue. Buber cites Jesus as an example of faith. Jesus points to the door that opens for us here and now and this is emunah, the Hebrew word for trust and confidence. Jesus trusted in God, the Father and he calls us to live our lives in trust and service before God. He offered the gift of his life to God the Father and suffered for the good of all (Origin and Meaning of Hasidism, p. 245, 247-248). Here Buber as a Jew emphasises the Jewishness of Jesus.

For Buber God can only be encountered as 'Thou'. The only possible relation with God is that of the I to the eternal Thou (Eclipse of God, p. 128). Buber's categories help us situate Thérèse's relation to Jesus. She experienced many 'I-Thou' relationships based on love, but gradually she was led away from him. She grew more and more to love the 'Thou' of Jesus. She discovered the Thou of Jesus in personal encounter by God's empowering spirit. She meditated on the words of scripture. This is all the more remarkable when one considers how few scriptural resources there were in the Carmel of Lisieux. She was inspired at an early stage by the "Imitation of Christ" and the works of St. John of the Cross became her spiritual nourishment. Her sacrifices show her trying to go beyond herself so that she could love purely. She offered herself with confidence to God the Father to allow him to accomplish his will of love. God in Jesus was a real Thou with whom she had a loving encounter and she offered herself with him to God the Father and offered herself to help others with her prayer and suffering.

Her 'Little Way' offers a way to enter this loving relationship - we will see this later. So many people feel excluded from a loving 'I-Thou' relationship of any kind that her way is a way of healing. Many of us are made feel worthless - the 'It' of Buber - that her way of love offers us a new perspective and an opening to a new way of life.

Thérèse describes her experience of love when she encountered the Thou of Jesus at her first communion.

The "beautiful day of days" finally arrived. The smallest details of that heavenly day have left unspeakable memories in my soul! The joyous awakening at dawn, the respectful embraces of the teachers and our (35r°) older companions! The large room filled with snow-white dresses in which each child was to be clothed in her turn! Above all, the procession into the chapel and the singing of the morning hymn: "O altar of God, where the angels are hovering!"

I don't want to enter into detail here. There are certain things that lose their perfume as soon as they are exposed to the air; there are deep spiritual thoughts that cannot be expressed in human language without losing their intimate and heavenly meaning; they are similar to ". . . the white stone I will give to him who conquers, with a name written on the stone which no one KNOWS except HIM who receives it."   (Rev 2:17)

Ah! How sweet was that first kiss of Jesus! It was a kiss of love; I felt that I was loved, and I said: "I love You, and I give myself to You forever!" There were no demands made, no struggles, no sacrifices; for a long time now Jesus and poor little Thérèse looked at and understood each other. That day, it was no longer simply a look, it was a fusion; they were no longer two, Thérèse had vanished as a drop of water is lost in the immensity of the ocean. Jesus alone remained; He was the Master, the King. Had not Thérèse asked Him to take away her liberty, for her liberty frightened her? She felt so feeble and fragile that she wanted to be united forever to the divine strength!   (MsA, 35 r°)

We already looked at the idea of the face to face encounter Thérèse had when she meditated on the image of the suffering Jesus. She saw that this face showed the fullness of Jesus' love. He underwent suffering in a world that did not understand him and rejected him. Yet he turns his face of love to this world. She tells her sister Céline that Jesus is on fire with love for us and she tells her to look at his face. "There you will see how He loves us" (LT 87).

Later in another letter she advises Céline: "Let us make our life a continual sacrifice, a martyrdom of love, a sigh, but a look and a sigh that are for him alone. . ." (LT 96). Thérèse is entering into a deeper 'I-Thou' loving relationship with Jesus.

Her contemplation of Jesus as the suffering servant (cf Is 53) leads her to see that her sufferings are one with his and are offered so that others may be healed and find peace in God. In a letter in 1891 to Céline she says: "Ah, Céline . . . Three years ago our souls had not yet been broken: happiness was still possible for us on earth, but Jesus cast a glance of love on us, a glance veiled in tears and this glance has become for us an ocean of suffering, but also an ocean of graces and love. . .(LT 127).

Thérèse and her family were distressed by the suffering of their father Louis and Thérèse was more and more in union with the suffering servant, Jesus. In a letter that year to Céline she emphasises that we must keep our gaze fixed on Jesus (LT 134). She knew the danger of self-seeking and not loving the Thou of Jesus. In the book of the Final Conversations we have the following testimony of Agnes on Thérèse beholding the 'face' of her beloved:

Her bed was no longer in the centre of the infirmary, but at the end of the room in a corner. To celebrate the feast of the following day, August 6, feast of the Transfiguration, we took from the choir the picture of the Holy face she so much loved and hung it on the wall to the right, decorating it with flowers and lights. She said, looking at the picture:

> "How well Our Lord did to lower His eyes when He gave us His
> portrait! Since the eyes are the mirror of the soul, if we had seen
> His soul, we would have died from joy.

"Oh! How much good that Holy Face has done me in my life! When I was composing my canticle: 'Vivre d'amour,' it helped me to do it with great ease. I wrote from memory, during my night silence, the fifteen couplets that I had composed during the day without a rough draft. That same day, when going to the refectory after the examination of conscience, I had just composed the St:

> To live from love is to dry Your Face,
> It's to obtain pardon for sinners.

"I repeated this to Him while passing by, doing so with great love. When looking at the picture, I cried out of love."   (DE, 5.8.7)

Here Thérèse brings to mind part of the poem the Spiritual Canticle composed by St. John of the Cross (+1591). Thérèse's beloved teacher:

"When thou didst look upon me,
Thine eyes imprinted upon me thy grace,
For this cause didst thou love me greatly.
Whereby mine eyes deserved to adore
that which they saw in thee."   (Spiritual Canticle, A, 23, 1)

In his commentary on the canticle, John tells us:

"For the sickness of love
 is not cured
except by your very presence and image."

. . . The reason for this is that the love of God is the soul's health
and the soul does not have full health until love is complete.
Sickness is nothing but the lack of health and when the soul does
not even have a single degree of love, she is dead. But when she
possesses some degrees of love of God, no matter how few, she is
then alive, yet very weak and infirm because of her little love. In
the measure that love increases she will be healthier and when
love is perfect she will have full health.
     (Spiritual Canticle, 11:11)

Thérèse gave herself for love of this love and to lead souls to the life of love
with God in which is our true health.

The Mystery of Jesus

Thérèse tells us: Jesus has no need of books or teachers to instruct souls; He
teaches without the noise of words. Never have I heard him speak, but I feel
that He is within me at each moment; He is guiding and inspiring me at each
moment (MsA, 83v°). In the Gospel of John Jesus had promised

"Anyone who loves me will keep my word
And my Father will love him,
And we shall come to him
And make a home in him"   (Jn 14:23)

God's presence is mediated by the power of the Holy Spirit which Jesus
promised to those who meditated on his word (Jn 14:13-18). Jesus lived this
message in her life and prayer. Jesus is the Word made flesh (Jn 1:14) and
Thérèse had a profound union with Him. He is not now seen as he was in the

streets of Nazareth and Jerusalem. He is 'hidden' in the words of scripture, by which we have in faith access to him and his message and in the sacraments. He is also present in a hidden way in our sufferings.

When he is hidden and silent the hardest trial of faith is to persevere, to endure in silence or with tears, unsure of the outcome, guided only by a small still voice telling us that we are God's servants and in the end our tears will cease and bring life and healing to others. We are asked to share Jesus' loneliness in Gethsemane and in faith allow him to bring the fruits of new life, healing and salvation.

Thérèse wrote about this 'hiddeness' to Céline who, at the time before her entry into Carmel, was enduring the dark night of her own suffering and confusion. In a letter from August 2nd, 1893 she says:

Dear little Céline

Your letter filled me with consolation. The road on which you are walking is a royal road, it is not a beaten track, but a path traced out by Jesus Himself. The spouse of the Canticles says that, not having found her Beloved in her bed, she arose to look for Him in the city but in vain; after having gone out of the city, she found Him whom her soul loved!... Jesus does not will that we find His adorable presence in repose; He hides Himself; He wraps Himself in darkness. It was not thus that He acted with the crowd of Jews, for we see in the gospel that the people were CARRIED AWAY when He was speaking. Jesus used to charm weak souls with His divine words, He was trying to make them strong for the day of trial. . . . But how small was the number of Our Lord's friends when He was SILENT before His judges! He made Himself poor that we might be able to give Him love. He holds out His hand to us like a beggar so that on the radiant day of judgment when He will appear in His glory, He may have us hear those sweet words: "Come, blessed of my Father, for I was hungry and you gave me to eat; I was thirsty, and you gave me to drink; I did not know where to lodge, and you gave me a home. I was in prison, sick, and you helped me." It is Jesus Himself who spoke those words; it is He who wants our love, who begs for it . . . . He places Himself, so to speak, at our mercy, He does not want to take anything unless we give it to Him, and the smallest thing is precious in His divine eyes. . . .

Dear Céline, let us take delight in our lot, it is so beautiful. Let us
give, let us give to Jesus; let us be miserly with others but prodigal
with Him.   (LT 145)

She goes on to say that Jesus is a 'hidden' treasure. In the end He Himself
'must be our reward'. Our health and wholeness consists in our union with God
in love - the fullness of which is now 'hidden' from us.

In her final days Thérèse reflected on how Jesus remained hidden in suffering.
She quotes Isaiah 53 saying there was no beauty in the suffering servant. This
was the basis of her devotion to the Holy Face or as she says 'to express it
better, the foundation of my piety. I, too, have desired to be without beauty,
alone in treading the winepress, unknown to everyone (DE, 5.8.9).

She was influenced by her teacher John of the Cross in meditating on Jesus'
hiddeness. In the first Stanza of the Spiritual Canticle John says:

"Where have you hidden,
Beloved, and left me moaning.
You fled like the stag
after wounding me,
I went out calling, but you were gone."

He goes on in his commentary to explain that the soul, enamoured of the Word,
the Son of God longs for union with him through clear and essential vision.

She goes out to achieve this union and yet suffers her beloveds' absence. He
desires total union with Christ in the first five Stanzas.

Yet the beloved remains hidden.
John wrote "Where have you hidden?"

This is like saying: O Word, my Spouse, show me where you are hidden. In
her petition she seeks the manifestation of his divine essence, because the
hiding place of the Word of God is, as St. John asserts (Jn. 1:18), the bosom of
the Father, that is, the divine essence, which is alien to every mortal eye and
hidden from every human intellect. Isaiah proclaimed in speaking to God:
Indeed, you are a hidden God (Is 45:15).

It is noteworthy however elevated God's communications and the experiences
of his presence are, and however sublime a person's knowledge of him may be,
these are not God essentially, nor are they comparable to him because, indeed,

he is still hidden to the soul. Hence, regardless of all these lofty experiences, a person should think of him as hidden and seek him as one who is hidden, saying: "Where have You hidden?"

Jesus is hidden in the person of the Father. He is one with the Father in the unity of the Holy Spirit. We have not yet arrived at our heavenly homeland. We do see clearly as yet. In the words of St. Paul "For, now, we see in a mirror, daily but then we will see face to face. Now I know only in part; then I shall know fully, even as I here have fully known. And now faith, hope and love abide, these three: and the greatest of these is love (1 Cor 13:12f).

We live in the 'in-between' time after Jesus' death and resurrection but before the inauguration of the new Heavenly Kingdom. We live here by faith, life and love and allow God work his secret purposes. Thérèse's vocation was to be love in the heart of the church (MsB, 3r°-v°). This was no easy vocation. A negative view of God kept his love from people's eyes. Fear had cast out love in so many quarters. Love is not loved. Thérèse's revolution has just begun. Thérèse saw during the time of Louis' illness that in the end Jesus himself would be the reward in a face-to-face encounter. He now shows himself as a humble beggar asking for love. He is present in all who suffer and in our brothers and sisters. This is why Thérèse spoke of sacrificing herself for her sisters, especially the ones others avoided. Here was Jesus.

In the early Church the early Fathers and Mothers went to the desert to pray. For Thérèse Carmel was such a desert in the modern world (MsA 25v°, 26v°). Thérèse describes how Jesus entered into a covenant with her and she became His own (MsA, 47r°). Thérèse had a deep devotion to Jesus present in the Blessed Sacrament. In one of her poems, Vivre d'amour, (Living on Love, PN 17), she speaks of the indwelling love of the Trinity. She describes the Eucharistic presence in the following verse:

> "Living on love is living on your life,
> Glorious King, delight of the elect.
> You live for me, hidden in a host.
> I want to hide myself for you, O Jesus!
> Lovers must have solitude,
> A heart to heart lasting night and day,
> Just one glance of yours makes my beatitude
> I live on love. . . ."

Here she shows her longing to love Jesus truly and not have any self-centredness in this. Here she was influenced by "The Imitation of Christ" which encourages self-forgetfulness so that our love may be pure.

In a later poem she sees a parallel in faith between the future glory of Heaven and the presence of Jesus in the Blessed Sacrament, here and now. She says:

"Heaven for me is hidden a little host
Where Jesus my spouse is veiled for love.
I go to the Divine Furnace to draw out life,
And there my sweet saviour listens to me night and day
Oh! What a happy moment when in your tenderness
You came, my Beloved, to transform me into yourself
That union of love, that ineffable intoxication
That is Heaven for me"

(PN 32, v. 3)

Thérèse became one with Jesus and she shared his love and compassion for the broken and those in need of mercy. She, like St. Francis, longed to feel this love and suffer with Jesus so that life may come to others, those who appear far away but yet in God's eyes are deeply loved. Francis had the stigmata in the flesh. Thérèse in the last eighteen months of her life suffered a stigmata of the spirit. She had trials of faith and spirit.

She was taunted by voices that made her doubt Heaven, herself and all she had given her life for. She tells us that the voices mock her about 'dreaming about the light, about a fatherland embalmed in the sweetest perfumes. You are dreaming about the eternal possession of the Creator of these marvels; you believe that one day you will walk out of this fog that surrounds you! Advance, advance; rejoice in death which will give you not what you hope for but a night still more profound, the night of nothingness" (MsC, 6v°). She had wondered why Atheists thought as they did. Now that Jesus had 'hidden' his presence she realised what Atheists suffered in their doubt (MsC, 5v°). She now sits at their table and prays for them as their sister. She was one with Jesus who bore the brokeness of all in his loneliness of Gethsemane, including Atheists. She shared his lonely night. She knew the inner meaning of Jesus' words: "Greater love than this is man has than he lay down his life for his friends" (Jn 15:12 quoted in MsC, 12r°). Her long agony in the last eighteen months of her life was a profound union with Jesus' lonely vigil and prayer for sinners, the weak and the broken and those who feel far from God. Living for love involves the total giving of oneself for love of all in Jesus.

Hans Urs Von Balthasar says all the mysticism of 'abyss' and the 'heart of God' is seen inevitably as a true mysticism of the cross, a mysticism of a sharing in the helplessness of the Word of God. In this way it has a place in the Church (A Theological Anthropology, p. 282). John of the Cross says that: "Union with God does not consist in recreation, experiences or spiritual feelings, but in the one and only living, sensory and spiritual, exterior and interior, death of the Cross (Ascent of Mount Carmel, ii, 7, 8-11). But suffering with Jesus who is hidden are the birth pangs for God's new-creation which Jesus began in his resurrection and the Holy Spirit poured out on us is the first down payment of the new Creation. In the present Thérèse suffers in solidarity with others. Here solidarity means: being solitary like, and with others. This was Jesus' prayer in Gethsemane where he suffered in solidarity with the brokeness of us all. Thérèse shares his lonely prayer. God selects certain souls to be with him and bring consolation to Him and a broken world. God's dream is that the Heart of Darkness be overcome by the Heart of Love.

In the "Diary of a Country Priest", George Bernanos catches this moment of union with the lonely Christ in the following reflection of the Curé in his diary:

> The truth is that I've always been in the Garden of Olives. And at the moment - yes. It's strange - at the very moment when he puts his hand on Peter's shoulder and asks the question - the very useless and almost naïve but oh so courteous and tender question - Are you sleeping? . . . I opened my mouth and was going to answer, but I couldn't. Too bad! Is it not enough that today, through the mouth of my old friend and counsellor, our Lord has done me the grace of revealing to me that nothing would ever snatch me from the place chosen for me from all eternity, my position as prisoner of the Holy Agony?   (Curé, p. 222)

Jesus and Thérèse whom he called lived out the words of the prophet Isaiah, describing the suffering servant:

> "Yet ours were the sufferings
> he was becoming,
> ours the sorrows he was carrying . . "   (Is 53:4)

Chapter Four

Abandonment to Love

The French word 'abandon', which we translate as abandonment, means in spirituality the giving of oneself totally to God in love and let him accomplish his will in us. John of the Cross in his "Ascent of Mount Carmel" tells us to leave all and find our treasure in God alone (Ascent, 1,13).

Thérèse had a happy year in 1867. She had many moments when she spoke with Celine and was filled with love for God. She says: "Passing by me, Jesus saw the time had come for me to be loved, He entered into a covenant with me. . ." (MsA, 47r°). Thérèse wanted to love Jesus with a passion (MsA, 47v°).

One Sunday in July, at the end of mass a picture of Jesus crucified slipped from her missal. No one was collecting the blood he had shed. Thérèse decided that she would henceforth remain, in spirit, at the foot of that cross to collect that blood for sinners. Charity entered into my heart. She too would be a fisher of human beings. She thirsted like Jesus. Her vocation to Carmel became clear and deep. She felt the need to forget herself. The Pranzini affair provided her with the opportunity to put her desires into practice.   (see MsA, 45°)

This led to her prayer and sacrifice as we saw for Pranzini.

She continues to tell us how she meditated on the cross of Jesus. As she contemplated the cross she says:

> I felt charity enter into my soul, and the need to forget myself and to please others; since then I've been happy! One Sunday, looking at a picture of Our Lord on the Cross, I was struck by the blood flowing from one of the divine hands. I felt a great pang of sorrow when thinking this blood was falling to the ground without anyone's hastening to gather it up. I was resolved to remain in spirit at the foot of the Cross and to receive the divine dew. I understood I was then to pour it out upon souls. The cry of Jesus on the Cross sounded continually in my heart: "I thirst!" These words ignited within me an unknown and very living fire. I wanted to give my Beloved to drink and I felt myself consumed

with a thirst for souls. As yet, it was not the souls of priests that attracted me, but those of great sinners; I burned with the desire to snatch them from the eternal flames.

Later when she would enter Carmel she wrote the following poem where she says:

"You, the Great God whom all Heaven adores,
You live in me, my Prisoner night and day,
Constantly your sweet voice implores me.
You repeat: "I thirst. . . I thirst for love, , ," (PN 31:5).

Jesus knew she was loved by Jesus, by a love that passes all understanding. She was now beginning a journey to give herself to love. There was a trial that anointed her first steps which would lead her on the road to abandonment. This was the fate of her father, Louis.

The Trial of Faith of Louis:

Louis Martin was a kind and loving father whom Thérèse adored. He was her king. She used to like to go on walks with Louis and their dog Tom. They went fishing together, visited the local churches and Louis brought the family to see the sea - a scene which enthralled the young Thérèse. Yet in MsA, 21r° Thérèse recounts a strange vision she had of her father suffering and his head covered. She cried out and Pauline, Céline, Léonie and Marie consoled her. It was only later they would learn the meaning of the vision.

At the end of the magical year 1887 she confided to Louis that she wished to enter Carmel. Her tears mingled with his (MsA, 49r°). He had already given two daughters to Carmel - Pauline and Marie. Now he was to lose his little queen. However she is too young. Thérèse conceived of the idea of having recourse to the Pope, during a pilgrimage to Rome. On their way to Rome they stop in Paris where she prayed at the Church of Our Lady of Victories. She realised that the 'smile of Our Lady' was genuine and her doubts were dispelled. She came to understand better the maternal love of Mary. She says: "I understood she was watching over me, that I was her child, and I could no longer give her any other name but Mamma for this seemed even so much more tender than mother. . ." (MsA, 56v°-57r°). In a letter from Paris she says: "I was very happy at Our Lady of Victories" (LT 30, Nov 6 Paris).

Her contact with priests led her to see their weaknesses all their 'extreme need for prayers,' since they always remain 'weak and fragile' (MsA, 56r°). She also was set on the road to 'abandon'. Her recourse to the Pope, her only plan of salvation (MsA, 62r°) was a failure. It is now her faith in God is called upon. She says: "I have such a great confidence in Him (God) that he will not be able to abandon me; I'm leaving everything in His hands" (LT 32). For her the cross is her portion.

Interiorly, how does she greet the bitter disappointment? "At the bottom of my heart I felt a great peace, since I had done absolutely everything in my power to respond to what God was asking of me; but this peace was only at the bottom and bitterness filled my soul, for Jesus was silent. He seemed to be absent and nothing revealed His presence to me" (MsA, 64r°). Let us listen also to her confession on the day of the failure: "Oh! Pauline, I cannot tell you what I felt. I was crushed, I felt abandoned, and, then, I am so far, so far. . . .I was crying a lot while writing this letter; my heart is very heavy. However, God cannot give me trials that are beyond my strength. . . .I have only God, Him only, Him alone!" (LT 36).

This is the time she is called to abandonment. She compared herself to a toy in Jesus the child's hands, but she believes one day Jesus will pick the 'toy' up for himself forever (MsA, 64r°-v°). She becomes capable of hoping against all hope (MsA, 64v°). Eventually her trust is rewarded and she is allowed to enter Carmel in 1888. Later on in Carmel, in July 1897, Thérèse wrote a letter to her 'spiritual child' Abbé Bellière. He was one of the priests her prioress asked her to write to give them courage. She speaks of her father, Louis, and mother, Zélie, in the letter. She says:

> God gave me a father and a mother more worthy of heaven than of earth; they asked the Lord to give them many children and to take them for Himself. This desire was answered: four little angels flew away to heaven, and five children left in the arena took Jesus for Bridegroom. It was with heroic courage that my father, like a new Abraham, climbed three times the mountain of Carmel to immolate to God what was most dear to him. First, there were his two eldest; then the third of his daughters, on the advice of her director and conducted by our incomparable father, made an attempt in the convent of the Visitation. (God was content with her acceptance, later she returned to the world where she lives as though in the

cloister). There remained to the Elect of God only two children, one eighteen years old, the other fourteen. The latter, "the little Thérèse," asked permission to fly to Carmel, which she obtained from her good father, who pushed his condescension even to taking her first to Bayeux, then to Rome, in order to remove the obstacles which were holding back the immolation of her whom he called his queen. When he had brought her to port, he said to the only child who remained with him: "If you want to follow the example of your sisters, I consent to it, do not worry about me." The angel who was to support the old age of such a saint answered that, after his departure for heaven, she would also fly to the cloister, which filled with joy him who lived only for God. But such a beautiful life was to be crowned by a trial worthy of it. A short time after my departure, the father whom we cherished with such good reason was seized with an attack of paralysis in his limbs, which was repeated several times, but it could not remain there, the trial would have been too sweet, for the heroic Patriarch had offered himself as a victim to God; so the paralysis, changing its course, settled in the venerable head of the victim whom the Lord had accepted. . . .I lack the space to give you some touching details. I want only to tell you that we had to drink the chalice to its very dregs and to separate ourselves for three years from our venerated father, entrusting him to religious but strange hands. He accepted this trial, the entire humiliation of which he understood, and he pushed heroism even to not willing that we ask for his cure.   (LT 261)

Louis' Last Agony:

As we can see from Thérèse's letter to Abbé Bellière that Louis suffered a lot in his final years. He was overcome by paralysis and depression. He had to be hospitalised in Caen.

For Thérèse on the day she took the veil, "Everything was sadness and bitterness. Nevertheless peace, always peace reigned at the bottom of the chalice" (MsA, 77r°). On this day the young Carmelite felt very weak and vulnerable.

What was the reason for Louis' turmoil? People said it was the loss of his daughters to Carmel that caused him to break down. Yet Celine who became sister Geneviève spoke later about how her father had felt in May 1888 that he had not done enough for God. He offered himself as a victim soul to be a consolation to others (see S. Piat, Histoire d'une famille, p. 363-406). When Louis prayed he felt an influx of peace and love but felt called to be with Jesus in his agony. Would Louis have been ill anyway? We do not know but we do know he offered his sufferings to be in union with Jesus in his loneliness. Grace works on nature.

This vocation was called 'victim-souls' one time, but now we speak more about the 'suffering servant'. The book of Deutero-Isaiah was written to comfort a broken people. A servant was chosen. He was described in chapter 42 in the following way:

Here is my servant whom I uphold, my chosen one
in whom my soul delights.
I have sent my spirit upon him,
he will bring fair judgement to the nations.
He does not cry out or raise his voice,
his voice is not heard in the street;
he does not break the crushed reed
or snuff the faltering wick.
Faithfully he presents fair judgement;
he will not grow faint,
he will not be crushed
until he has established
fair judgement on earth,
and the coasts and islands
are waiting for his instruction.   (Is 42:1-4)

The servant is the gentle one that heals the people but a shock is in store when it is shown that the servant is the one whose suffering redeems the people. In Isaiah 53 we read of the servant's suffering:

Who has given credence
to what we have heard?
And who has seen in it
a revelation of Yahweh's arm?
Like a sapling he grew up before him,
like a root in arid ground.

He had no form or charm to attract us,
no beauty to win our hearts;
he was despised, the lowest of men,
a man of sorrows, familiar with suffering,
one man from whom, as it were,
we averted our gaze,
despised, for whom we had no regard. (Is 53:1-3)

The individual servants suffering and death was on Israel's behalf and on behalf of the nations. His suffering was redemptive. In the next set of verses the prophet tells us who the servant suffered for.

"Yet ours were the sufferings
he was bearing,
ours the sorrows he was carrying,
while we thought of him
as someone being punished
and struck with affliction by God;
whereas he was being wounded
for our rebellions,
crushed because of our guilt;
the punishment reconciling us fell on him,
and we have been healed by his bruises.
We had all gone astray like sheep,
each taking his own way,
and Yahweh brought the acts of rebellion
of all of us to bear on him.
Ill-treated and afflicted,
he never opened his mouth,
like a lamb led to the slaughter-house,
 like a sheep dumb before its shearers
he never opened his mouth. (Is 53:4-7)

It is in his suffering that others are healed. To the world in its wisdom the servant appears just like Louis and later his little Thérèse. They appear broken, ill and appear to be rejected by God. Yet they are in union with the suffering servant who in Jesus and by their wounds are healed. In the poem we read of the servant in words spoken by God:

"By his knowledge, the upright one,
my servant will justify many
by taking their guilt on himself"   (Is 53:11)

In the end God justifies the suffering one. He calls him to himself:

Hence I shall give him a portion
with the many,
and he will share the booty
with the mighty,
for having exposed himself to death
and for being counted
as one of the rebellious,
whereas he was bearing the sin of many
and interceding for the rebellious.   (Is 53:12)

God's word is a word of healing and it achieves what it sets out to accomplish
(Is 55:11). Jesus lived the life of the suffering servant in his agony, and death.
Yet God showed he was present by raising Jesus from the dead and giving new
life to his people. In Paul's letter to the Philippians we read:

Who, being in the form of God,
did not count equality with God
something to be grasped.

But he emptied himself,
taking the form of a slave,
becoming as human beings are;
and being in every way
like a human being,
he was humbler yet,
even to accepting death,
death on a cross.

And for this God raised him high,
and gave him the name
which is above all other names;

So that all beings
in the heavens, on earth

and in the underworld,
should bend the knee at the name of Jesus
and that every tongue should acknowledge
Jesus Christ as Lord,
to the glory of God the Father.   (Phil 2:6-11)

Though Jesus was in the form of God he emptied himself of all power. The Greek word for this is kenoo and Jesus' self-emptying is called kenosis. He did not cling to power or royal status with God. He came as a servant and was crucified. In 1 Cor 1:21-24 we see how this act confounds the wisdom of this world. George Bernanos uses the term 'bien-pensants' (the right thinker) for those who think in 'worldly ways'. Yet God acts in his own way.

Jesus' sacrifice as servant and crucifixion are accepted by God who raises him up and shows his self-giving is greater than any. That is why he is given the name above all other names and all beings bend their knee at the name of Jesus.

Paul speaks of these when God calls in Jesus. He speaks of how he has come to know Christ and he wishes to follow him, "that I may come to know him and the power of the resurrection, and partake of his sufferings, by being moulded to the pattern of his death, striving towards the goal of the resurrection of the dead." (Phil 3:10) As St. Peter says: "by his wounds we are healed" (1 Pt 2:24). Jesus calls certain souls to be with him in his lonely agony as suffering servant. Louis was one.

Ten days after Thérèse's clothing, which had been like a great feast day of 'triumph' for her father, a tragic event occurred. M. Martin experienced a time of depression. He bought a revolver in order to protect his daughters. The doctor decided to hospitalise him. Then, a month after Thérèse of Lisieux's clothing, her father was taken forcibly to the hospital of Bon-Sauveur, in Caen, which accommodated over two thousand sick people. Céline and Léonie were upset about it. Their uncle confided to one of his particularly close friends the care they took to make M. Martin believe they were going to take a walk, and that was the confinement. M. Martin would remain there more than three years. Thérèse would have but a single parlour visit with her father. She would see him again only once between his admission to the hospital and his death, which would take place several months after that parlour visit, when, in his wheelchair, he could no longer speak, only make a gesture: "To heaven!" That was all.

(Histoire d'une âne, p. 136-137)

That had been heartrending for Thérèse, especially because everyone talked about it in Lisieux. There was gossip, and Thérèse would say nothing. People insinuated that the father's illness was perhaps due to the fact that his daughters had entered the Carmel. Thérèse was nineteen years old when her father left the hospital. Louis died in 1894.

Bernard Bro in his book on Thérèse left us the following reflection:

Permit me to mention here the visual shortcut that film maker Alain Cavalier used in his film Thérèse. Very strict about historical correctness, deeply esteemed by all the best experts on Thérèse of Lisieux, Cavalier depicted the hardness of this last parlour visit for Thérèse by superimposing several anecdotes. A tear having run down M. Martin's face, someone dries it with a little handkerchief. Thérèse asks her prioress for permission to keep it. The latter simply remarks that she already has a family souvenir: the pen tray in her writing box. Thérèse consents. She will not even have one of her father's tears to keep. The cinematic license transcribes well Thérèse's deep emotion.

(Bernard Bro, Thérèse of Lisieux, p. 51f)

Louis by his life and example taught Thérèse much. In a letter written on 26th April 1889 Thérèse reflected on how Jesus suffered. He suffered in sadness. She asked could a soul truly suffer without sadness. She thought of people wanting to suffer in some good manner. This was an illusion (LT 89). The suffering servant abandoned his fate and mission to God who had the power to work through his weakness. Jesus suffered as the suffering servant. Thérèse, like Louis, was called to be with him in his lonely hour and in this way bring healing to the world. This is the world of 'abandon', abandonment. It means confidence that the God of tenderness is working even in our sorrows and bringing healing to a broken world and its people. Thérèse says: "How I want to apply myself to doing the will of God with the greatest self-surrender (MsA, 84v°). Interestingly in 1938 Cardinal Eugenio Pacelli (later Pope Pius XII) said that Thérèse was the greatest healer of the twentieth century.

Céline had remained at home to look after Louis. Her friendship was very important for Thérèse and her growth. In a letter to Céline, on July 6th 1893, Thérèse wrote of Jesus: "who is my director. . . He teaches me to do all things through love, to refuse him nothing, to be content when he gives me a chance of proving to him that I love him. But this is done in peace, in abandonment, it is Jesus who is doing all in me, and I am doing nothing" (LT 142).

Part Two:

The Little Way of Love and Healing

Chapter One
Thérèse on the Way

"But why do I desire to communicate your secrets of love, O Jesus, for was it not you alone who taught them to me and can you not reveal them to others? Yes, I know it, and I beg you to do it. I beg you to cast your divine glance upon a great number of little souls. I beg you to choose a legion of little victims worthy of your love" (MsB, 5v°).

During this period Thérèse began to grow closer to Jesus and join him in his journey from Good Friday to Easter Sunday. We saw where Thérèse contemplated the picture of Jesus crucified and felt the gift of charity enter her soul. Charity is the gift of the Holy Spirit. Thérèse saw in this moment that Jesus' Paschal journey is always present to us in the human struggle against the heart of darkness. This grace that came to Thérèse is Eucharistic in that she refers to the spilling of Jesus' blood. Her insight showed her the divine Christ given over to the Cross, his 'thirst' for our faith and love, his 'thirst' to transform our love into his, his desire that all be saved, his 'thirst for souls.' The Eucharist makes these mysteries present here today. From now on she saw her mission as: "loving Jesus and making him loved. . ." (LT 96, 220, PN 6).

Thérèse said she felt charity enter into her soul as she contemplated the picture of the crucified one. She says pondering the blood that fell "I was resolved to remain in spirit at the foot of the Cross to receive the divine dew. I understood I was to pour it out upon souls" (MsA, 45v°).

Thérèse had read "The Imitation of Christ" by Thomas à Kempis. In 1887 she discovered the work of Abbé Charles Arminjon (1824-885), "Fin du monde présent et mystères de la vie future." She learned a lot from these books. She was also familiar with Dom Prosper Guéranger's, "The Liturgical Year." In the summer of 1887 Thérèse wished to read more and more "to love Jesus with passion, giving him a thousand proofs of my love while it was possible" (MsA, 47v°). She says that reading Arminjon's book was one of the greatest graces of her life and deepened her love and faith (MsA, 47v°).

Thérèse was even more eager to enter Carmel. She was frustrated in her quest to enter the convent. Conrad de Meester in his work, Dynamique de la

Confiance, pp. 157-168) shared that all the setbacks she suffered led her to 'abandon', to trust that God was ever active and she was confident her situation was in his hands. During this period she endured the opposition of her uncle Isidore Guerin, the interview with the Bishop Mgr. Hugonin, the opposition of M. Delatroette, the superior of Carmel and the failed attempt to get permission from Pope Leo XIII to enter Carmel. After the failed audience with the Pope she said "In the bottom of my heart I felt a great peace, since I had everything in my power to answer what God was asking of me. This peace, however, was in the depths only, bitterness filled my soul, for Jesus was silent" (MsA, 64r°). Her patience and 'abandon' won out. She entered Carmel in April 1888. She describes her vocation in the following passage:

> I have said that Jesus was "my director." Upon entering Carmel, I met one who was to serve me in this capacity, but hardly had I been number among his children when he left for exile. Thus, I came to know him only to be deprived of him. Reduced to receiving one letter a year from him to my twelve, my heart quickly turned to the Director of directors, and it was He who taught me that science hidden from the wise and prudent and revealed to little ones.   (Mt 11:25).
>
> The little flower transplanted to Mount Carmel was to expand under the shadow of the cross. The tears and blood of Jesus were to be her dew, and her Sun was His adorable Face veiled with tears. Until my coming to Carmel, I had never fathomed the depths of the treasures hidden in the Holy Face. It was through you, dear Mother, that I learned to know these treasures. Just as formerly you had preceded us into Carmel, so also you were first to enter deeply into the mysteries of love hidden in the Face of our Spouse. You called me and I understood. I understood what real glory was. He whose kingdom is not of this world showed me that true wisdom consists in "desiring to be unknown and counted as nothing," in "placing one's joy in the contempt of self." Ah! I desired that, like the Face of Jesus, "my face be truly hidden, that no one on earth would know me." I thirsted after suffering and I longed to be forgotten.
>
> How merciful is the way God has guided me. Never, has He given me the desire for anything which He has not given me, and even His bitter chalice seemed delightful to me.   (MsA, 71r°)

It was at this time that Louis Martin began his own way of the cross and his trial was also a great trial for Thérèse and the other Martin sisters. Thérèse saw in him the face of the 'suffering servant' and she began to call herself, "Thérèse de L'Enfant Jesus et de la Sainte Face" (Thérèse of the infant Jesus and the Holy Face). She had a little picture of the Holy Face which she kept above the place where she prayed. She was being led more and more into sharing with Jesus his Paschal journey - the Good Friday to Easter Sunday. She says that "Spiritual aridity was my daily bread, and deprived of all consolation, I was still the happiest of creatures since all my desires had been satisfied" (MsA, 73r°). During this time, her main reading was John of the Cross. Her main source of inspiration was Sacred Scripture. Carmel did not possess a full Bible. Thérèse meditated on scripture from the readings at mass. The readings from the Office, the Liturgy of the Hours were in Latin but the nuns gathered in the evening to hear the readings in French. When Céline joined in 1894 she brought with her a copy-book full of scriptural quotations. When one considers how meagre were her resources, it is staggering the insight Thérèse had into the Word of God. She saw scripture as inspired by the Holy Spirit and had a deep reverence for the Word of God and the Spirit of scripture.

Thérèse and Scripture

Jesus was Thérèse's inner teacher. This would seem to suggest that she might be one who claimed a 'gnosis', a special knowledge no-one else had. This was not true as any investigation of her writings will show. "God is Love" (1 Jn 4:8, 16) and Jesus calls this God his Father. "The Father and I are one" (Jn 10:30) says Jesus. The prologue of the gospel tells us

"No one has ever seen God,
it is the only Son,
who is close to the Father's heart,
who has made him known."   (Jn 1:18)

He who knows the heart of tenderness of God is Jesus who reveals this tenderness to us. All Jesus' life shows us this relation. He said he loved the Father and he acted like the Father had asked him (Jn 14:31). His food was to do the will of the one who sent him (Jn 4:34). In the end the world of darkness rejects Jesus who says, "Am I not to drink the cup the Father gives me" (Jn 18:11). In every instant of his life Jesus lived this life of love with his Father and he gives himself totally to God so that the world may have life. He knows he is loved totally by God who is all-love. He knows he is his son and in him we become children of God. The letter to the Ephesians expresses this:

"Thus he chose us in Christ,
before the world was made,
to be holy and faultless
before him in love,
making us after himself beforehand,
to be his adopted children
through Jesus Christ."   (Eph 1:4-5)

Jesus asked those he called to love one another as he loved them (Jn 15:12). He goes on to say: "No-one has greater love than to lay down his life for his friends."

"You are my friends,
if you do what I command you,
I shall no longer call you servants
because a servant does not know
the master's business.
I call you friends."   (Jn 15:12-15)

Jesus promises the gift of the Holy Spirit so we can love like him and begin to understand Jesus' words. Jesus also tells us that if we love him:

"Anyone who loves me will keep my word,
and my Father will love him,
and we shall come to him,
and make our home with him."   (Jn 14:23)

We are loved by God and are called to be one with him by being incorporated into the life of Christ by the Holy Spirit. Paul uses the expression 'in Christ' for this mystery. We are loved by God and our prayer is done in accordance with his will. Jesus tells us:

"I have loved you
just as the Father has loved me.
Remain in my love.

If you keep my covenant,
you will remain in my love,
just as I have kept
my Father's commandments
and remain in his love."   (Jn 15:9f)

'Remain in my love' is what Jesus calls us to do. We grow into God's love as we grow in the Spirit and allow God to heal us and make us new. We saw this in the early years of Thérèse's life as she left the way of her old childhood behind and became a new person. From now on she would lead us to a way of participating in Jesus' life of love with the Father. But we must wait a little before we come to the 'little way'. She looked at the great love of God that she experienced in her heart and seen in Jesus. The letter to the Ephesians reminds us:

"As God's dear children, then, take him
as your pattern and follow Christ by
loving as he loved you, giving himself
up for us as an offering and sweet smelling
sacrifice to God."   (Eph 5:1)

As we allow Jesus to enter our hearts we begin to change and certain souls like Thérèse begin to pray with Jesus' Spirit. They begin to share his heart of love and radiate that love to others. Thérèse cannot be understood on her own. She gave her life to God in Jesus and this relationship is key to understanding Thérèse.

In Paul's first letter the Corinthians that Christ was raised (egererthai, 15:4, 15:14) constitutes an essential part of the divine gift by grace alone. The new life theme is expressed as "but now you have been washed clean, you have been sanctified, and you have been justified in the name of the Lord Jesus Christ and through the Spirit of our God" (1 Cor 6:11). A great problem for the Corinthian community was power, status, acceptance and self-esteem. Anthony Thistleton interprets this part of Paul's letter in the following words:

This applies with particular poignancy to the addresses at Corinth. As we have noted, many were obsessed with problems arising from the thirst for status, acceptance and self-esteem. Paul declares: You are accepted! You belong! You have privileged status! But all this comes from God as his free, sovereign, gift. He tells them (to borrow Tillich's phrase) to accept that they are accepted as the antidote to the status hunger which drives them to compete, as long as they keep in mind the basis and ground of their acceptance. Justification by grace through faith fits the Corinthian situation no less readily than that of the readers of Galatians and Romans. It speaks equally to their cultural situation, where obsession with achievement and status and, no less, anxiety over low self-esteem compound the ills of society: "but by the grace of God I am what I am"

(A. Thistleton, 1 Corinthians, NIGTC, p. 547f)

Paul Tillich said that faith was the courage to accept acceptance (see Tillich, The Courage to Be, p.66). This is not Thérèsian language. Yet we can use it to understand Thérèse. In the time of the scruples she did not accept herself and she had yet to come to God who is totally loving. His love is pure gift. Thérèse had thought for a long time her faults and failings would distance her from God. In October 1891, Thérèse was uncertain and afraid. She said: "I was having great interior trials of all kinds, even to the point of asking myself whether heaven really existed. I felt disposed to say nothing of my interior dispositions since I didn't know how to express them, but I hardly entered the confessional when I felt my soul expand" (MsA, 80v°). This was during a retreat preached by Alexis Prou (1844-1914), a Franciscan from Caen. The retreat was conducted from the 8th to the 15th October 1891.

She was troubled in conscience believing it was terribly easy to offend God and it was easy to commit a mortal sin. Fr. Prou directed her towards the mercy of God which is pure grace and infinite. It is the expression of his love. She felt confidence to place herself as she was in the arms of God, the one who accepted her as she was - this included her smallness and weakness. She met Fr. Prou a number of times. In MsA she tells us of this graced encounter.

I had made a preparatory novena with great fervour, in spite of the inner sentiment I had, for it seemed to me that the preacher would not be able to understand me since he was supposed to do good to great sinners but not to religious souls. God wanted to show me that He was the Director of my soul, and so He made use of this Father specifically, who was appreciated only by me in the community. At the time I was having great interior trials of all kinds, even to the point of asking myself whether heaven really existed. I felt disposed to say nothing of my interior dispositions since I didn't know how to express them, but I had hardly entered the confessional when I felt my soul expand. After speaking only a few words, I was understood in a marvellous way and my soul was like a book in which this priest read better than I did myself. He launched me full sail upon the waves of confidence and love which so strongly attracted me, but upon which I dared not advance. He told me that my faults caused God no pain, and that holding as he did God's place, he was telling me in His name that God was very much pleased with me.

Oh! How happy I was to hear those consoling words! Never had I heard that our faults could not cause God any pain, and this assurance filled me with joy, helping me to bear patiently with life's exile. I felt at the bottom of my heart that this was really so, for God is more tender than a mother, and were you not, dear Mother, always ready to pardon the little offences I committed against you involuntarily? How often I experienced this! No word of reproach touched me as much as did one of your caresses. My nature was such that fear made me recoil; with love not only did I advance, I actually flew. (MsA, 80v°)

Thérèse spent many hours a day in prayer, at the mass, the Divine Office, Eucharistic adoration and meditation. She was now deeply in love with Jesus and her 'I-Thou' relationship was deepening all the time. When Thérèse spoke and wrote her words cannot be understood without reference to Jesus' words in sacred scripture. Her use of 'little' and 'bitterness' illustrate this.

Jesus warned his disciples about pride. They asked who is the greatest. So he called a little child among them. Then he said, "In truth I tell you, unless you change and become like little children you will never enter the kingdom of Heaven. And so the one who makes himself as this little child is the greatest in the kingdom of Heaven" (Mt 18:1-4).

In the gospel of Mark we see the scene where Jesus tells them of the sufferings he has to face. His words do not touch the disciples. Their hearts are set on position, prestige and power in the new kingdom. They do not hear the one who is suffering. Jesus tells them: "If anyone wants to be first, he must make himself last of all and servant of all! He then took a little child whom he had set among them and he embraced the child and said to them, "Anyone who welcomes a little child such as this in my name welcomes me; and anyone who welcomes me, welcomes not me but the one who sent me" (Mk 9:35-38).

Jesus emphasises the humility, truth and honesty of the little child (Mt 18:4). Jesus' love for the little ones is pushed up by the mothers of the little ones. We read: "Then people brought little children to him for him to lay his hands on them and pray" (Mt 19:13). The disciples still did not understand. They were locked into their own world with dreams of power and glory. They try to turn the children away. An important man like Jesus shouldn't have to bother with 'little ones' but Jesus said: "Let the children alone, and do not stop them from coming; for it is to such as these that the kingdom of Heaven belongs" Then he laid his hands on them and went his way (Mt 19:14f). All of this meant for Thérèse that it was love alone that was central (DE 29.6.9). God loved us in our weakness and she could as a 'little, poor one' give herself with her love to God. She was now to have confidence in God's infinite love and mercy and that, even though she felt weak, was loved and accepted. This gave her wings to continue on her journey to God.

Father Pichon and his letter to Thérèse

Father Pichon (1843-1919) had been her spiritual director of Marie, Thérèse's sister. In August 1883 he met Thérèse. He preached a retreat in the Carmel of Lisieux in October 1887, and again in May 1888 when Thérèse was a postulant. He was sent to Canada as a missionary (1884-1866; 1888-1907) and Thérèse corresponded with him. Father Pichon wrote to Thérèse in January 1893. We do not have any copies of Thérèse's letters to him but from Fr. Pichon's letter we can detect that scruples had still arisen in Thérèse's heart. Once again this letter grounds Thérèse in God's mercy. Our life with God is not something once and for all. It has to be tended, 'watered' and minded. We need to begin again many times.

Dear little Lamb of The Child Jesus,

I can see no longer except with four eyes! But my heart never loses sight of you, and our souls are forever inseparable in Jesus. You are really to be pitied if my silence is as painful to you as it is to me. You speak to me, and I am answering you in the adorable Heart of the Beloved. Do you understand me as I understand you? All the echoes of your soul are joyous to me.

What should I wish for you this year when the Sacred Heart of Jesus wills to be your Protector and your Patron. Is there any greater happiness than to be spoiled by the Heart of love?

Close to the Sacred Heart one sigh is very much; one sigh is sufficient for Him to open His Heart entirely to you. Dare, then, to complain again at having only a sigh!

Dear Child of my soul, listen to what I am about to tell you in the name and on the part of Our Lord: No, no, you have not committed any mortal sins. I swear it. No, we cannot sin gravely without knowing it. No, after absolution, we must not doubt about our state of grace. To your Mother St. Theresa, who was praying one day for souls, who were deluding themselves, Our Lord answered: "My daughter, no one is lost without knowing it perfectly." Banish, then, your worries. God wills it, and I command it. Take my word for it: Never, never, never, have you committed a mortal sin. Go quickly to kneel before the Tabernacle to thank Our Lord. Fall asleep, tranquil and serene in the arms of Jesus. He has never betrayed you; He will never betray you.   (LC 152)

The words of Fr. Prou and Fr. Pichon in the end released Thérèse and gave her the courage to abandon all into the hands of love and 'God is Love' (1 Jn 4:8, 16). The eyes of her heart and mind now see clearly that God is light and love. In 1925 when Pope Pius XI canonised Thérèse he called her a 'word of God' for today. She had allowed God's love to flow through her to many others. Thérèse will say later, in MsB, that Jesus "has no need of our works, but only of our love, for the same God declares. He has no need to tell us when He is hungry did not fear to beg for a little water from the Samaritan woman. He was thirsty. But when He said "give me to drink", it was the love of his poor creator, the creator of the universe was seeking. He was thirsty for love . . . He finds how hearts who surrender to this without reservations, who understand the real tenderness of his infinite love" (MsB, 1v°). In this way she showed us God's tenderness which was now real for her. She had moved from fear to love. Perfect love had cast out fear (cf 1 Jn 4:18). This is the word she spoke to a new generation.

The Quiet Years

The early years of Thérèse in Lisieux were the years in which Thérèse's union with Jesus deepened and where the little way of confidence and abandon, the little way of spiritual childhood began to take root. She entered Carmel without any illusions. She describes how suffering welcomed her into Carmel (MsA, 69v°). It was at this time that Louis entered his night of suffering. Thérèse describes how at her profession (1890) even though it was a time of sadness yet she felt a peace inside (MsA, 76v-77r°). Thérèse had special devotion to the infant Jesus, using this name in her religious life. In one of the pieces she wrote later for recreation among the nuns, she describes how the infant Jesus already looks to the cross (RP, 2,3r°). She joined together the face of Jesus in the child at Bethlehem and the face of the crucified one.

In a poem written in 1897 when she was suffering she offers herself and her illness to Jesus. To use Thérèse's language she describes herself as throwing herself at Jesus' feet, in an act of pure and total love. We discover in her "An Unpetalled Rose" (the title of her poem). She is not asking for anything, she abandons herself to his mercy. She addresses herself to The Child Jesus. She says:

> "For you, I must die, Child, Beauty Supreme,
> What a blessed fate!
> In being unpetalled, I want to prove to you that I love you.
> O my Treasure!. . .
> Under your baby steps, I want to live here below
> With mystery,
> And I'd like to soften once more on Calvary
> Your last steps! . . ."   (PN 51, 5)

Here we see the full flowering of Thérèse's thoughts on how the incarnation and the Paschal mystery are intrinsically linked. The eternal son of God reveals for Thérèse 'eternal innocence' and the 'supreme beauty' of the merciful Father (LT 220). In love Thérèse sees Jesus abandon all into the hands of the Father.

It was at this time that Céline and Léonie looked after their suffering father. Thérèse wrote to Céline who stayed in Caen where her father was hospitalised. "Let us suffer the little pain, without courage! . . . (Jesus suffered in sadness! Without sadness would the soul suffer!...) And still we would like to suffer generously, goodly! . . . Céline what an illusion! . . . We'd never want to fall? .

. . What does it matter, my Jesus, if I fall at each moment; I see my weakness through this and this is a great gain for me . . . You can see through this what I can do and now You will be more tempted to carry me in Your arms (LT 89, April 1889). She saw in the figure of her father, the suffering face of Jesus. In a letter written in July, 1889, to Céline: "Our dear Father must be much loved by Jesus to have to suffer this way" (LT 82). Later in the year Céline describes her worries and trials. Thérèse replies:

Jesus! . . .

Dear little Céline,

Your letter gave great sadness to my soul! Poor little Papa! . . . No, the thoughts of Jesus are not our thoughts, and His ways are not our ways . . . .
He is offering us a chalice as bitter as our feeble nature can bear! . . . Let us not withdraw our lips from this chalice prepared by the hand of Jesus . . . .
Let us see life as it really is . . . . It is a moment between two eternities . . . . Let us suffer in peace! . . .

I admit that this word peace seemed a little strong to me, but the other day, when reflecting on it, I found the secret of suffering in peace . . . . The one who says peace is not saying joy, or at least, felt joy . . . . To suffer in peace it is enough to will all that Jesus wills . . . . To be the spouse of Jesus we must resemble Jesus, and Jesus is all bloody, He is crowned with thorns! . . .
"A thousand years in your eyes, Lord, as are yesterday, which has PASSED" . . .

"On the banks of the river of Babylon, we sat and wept when we remembered Sion . . . . We hung our harps on the willows in the fields . . . Those who led us into captivity said to us: 'Sing for us one of the pleasant songs from Sion.' How could we sing the song of the Lord in a foreign land!" . . . Psalm of David . . . .

No, let us not sing the canticles of heaven to creatures . . . . But like Cecilia, let us sing a melodious canticle in our heart to our Beloved! . . .

The canticle of suffering united to His sufferings is what delights His Heart the most! . . .

Jesus is on fire with love for us . . . Look at His adorable Face! . . . Look at His eyes lifeless and lowered! Look at His wounds . . . . Look at Jesus in His Face . . . . There you will see how He loves us.

Sister Thérèse of The Child Jesus of the Holy Face

(LT 87)

Thérèse enters more into the mystery of the suffering when she meditates on the text of Is 53. Over the years she will quote this passage 19 times. The first mention is found in letter 108, 1890. Thérèse comes to see Jesus as the suffering servant and her father shares with Jesus in his ministry as suffering servant. She says in her letter:

Céline, it's such a long time ago . . . And already the soul of the prophet Isaiah was immersed, just as our own soul is, in the HIDDEN BEAUTIES of Jesus . . . Ah, Céline, when I read these things, I wonder what time really is? . . . Time is only a mirage, a dream . . . Already God sees us in glory, He TAKES DELIGHT in our eternal beatitude! Ah! What good this thought does my soul, and I understand now why He is not bargaining with us . . . . He feels that we understand Him, and He is treating us as His friends, as His dearest spouses. . . .

Céline, since Jesus was (alone in treading the wine) which He is giving us to drink, let us not refuse in our turn to wear clothing stained in blood . . . Let us tread for Jesus a new wine which may quench His thirst, which will return Him love for love . . . And, then, looking about, He will see that we are coming to help Him! . . . His face was as though hidden! . . . Céline, it is still hidden today, for who understands the tears of Jesus? . . .

Dear Céline, let us make a little tabernacle in our heart where Jesus may take refuge, and then He will be consoled, and He will forget what we cannot forget: (the ingratitude of souls that abandon Him in a deserted tabernacle! . . .)

(Open to me, my sister, my beloved, for my face is covered with dew, my locks with the drops of night) (cant. Of cant.). That is what Jesus says to our soul when He is abandoned and forgotten! . . . Céline, forgetfulness, it seems to me that it's this which causes Him the greatest sorrow! . . .

Papa! . . . Ah, Céline, I cannot tell you all I am thinking, it would take too long, and how say things that the mind itself can hardly express, deep things that are in the innermost recesses of the soul! . . . (LT 108, July 1890)

At the end of the letter Thérèse quotes from the prophet Isaiah, chapter 53 even though she does mix in other parts of Isaiah (Is 63:1-5). Nevertheless this shows Thérèse's deeper penetration into the mystery of suffering. It is not the suffering that she praises but the spirit of love that enables Jesus to carry that suffering and redeem others. He enters into our misery to heal us and lead us out of that misery. She spoke to Céline in an earlier letter about her vocation and Céline's. They were soul-sisters. Thérèse says:

My dear Céline,

If you only knew how you touched the heart of your Thérèse! . . . Your little flowerpots are DELIGHTFUL, and you DON'T KNOW the pleasure they gave me! . . . Céline . . . . Your letter pleased me very much; I felt how much our souls were made to understand each other, and to walk by the same way! . . .Life . . . Ah, it's true, for us it has no more attraction . . . But I am mistaken. It's true that the attractions of this world have vanished for us, but this is only a smoke . . . And the reality remains for us. Yes, life is a treasure . . . Each moment is an eternity, an eternity of joy in heaven, an eternity of seeing God face to face, of being one with Him! . . . There is only Jesus who is; all the rest is not . . . . Let us love Him, then, unto folly; let us save souls for Him. Ah! Céline, I feel that Jesus is asking both of us to quench His thirst by giving Him souls, the souls of priests especially. I feel that Jesus wills that I say this to you, for our mission is to forget ourselves and to reduce ourselves to nothing . . . . We are so insignificant . . . And yet Jesus wills that the salvation of souls depends the sacrifices of our love. He is begging souls from us . . . . Ah, let us understand

His look! There are so few who understand it. Jesus is giving us the remarkable grace of instructing us Himself and of showing us a hidden light! . . . Céline . . . Life will be short, eternity is without end . . . . Let us make our life a continual sacrifice, a martyrdom of love, in order to console Jesus. He wants only a look, a sigh, but a look and a sigh that are for Him alone! . . . . Let all the moments of our life be for Him alone; let creatures touch us only in passing. There is only one thing to do during the night, the one night of life which will come only once, and this is to love, to love Jesus with all the strength of our heart and to save souls for Him so that He may be loved . . . . Oh, make Jesus loved! Céline! How easily I talk with you . . . It's as if I were speaking to my soul . . . . Céline, it seems to me that I can say everything to you . . . .

(Thank you again for your pretty jars; little Jesus is radiant when He is so well adorned.)

The shape of her vocation is beginning to take shape. She understands that Jesus is calling her to share in his work of bringing light to a darkened world. This is why she offers herself in a 'martyrdom of love, in order to console Jesus'. Her prayer and her life which is a living prayer become one with Jesus.

Thérèse spoke of Jesus' thirst in another letter to Céline. She says of Jesus: "He has so much need of love and He is so thirsty that he expects from us the drop of water that must refresh him" (LT 107, May 1890). Jesus' thirst is for love and the salvation of all people. We can offer our hearts in love to him and seek his will in the healing of the world. He calls us to share in his work. Here we see the beginnings of the 'Little Way'.

In the family trial that was the suffering of Louis, Thérèse discerns the hidden work of Jesus who accomplishes his work in mysterious ways. This letter was written just before her profession on September 24, 1890. An eye witness of her profession, V. Lahaye, said: "Her eyes had a light by candour and purity, but on this morning and decisive occasions their material goodness gave way to a certain seriousness" (Souvenirs d'un témoin aux cérémonies de Vêtre et de Profession). Yet in spite of tears and disappointment Thérèse says "It is Jesus who is conducting this affair, it is He, and I recognised His touch of love."

Later she says:

Today's trial is a difficult sorrow to understand. We see a joy which is offered to us; it's possible, natural. We extend our hand . . . And we cannot grasp this consolation so much desired . . . . But, Céline, how mysterious all this is! . . . We no longer have a home here below, or, at least, you can say just as the Blessed Virgin did: "What a home." Yes, what a home . . . But it's not a human hand that has does this, it's Jesus. It is His veiled look that has fallen upon us! . . . I received a letter from our exiled Father, and here is one passage from it: "Oh! My alleluia is filled with tears. Neither one of your Fathers will be there to offer you to Jesus. Must you complain very much here below when the angels up above congratulate you and the saints envy you. It's your crown of thorns that makes them jealous. Love, then, its stings as so many proofs of love from the divine spouse."

Céline, let us accept with a good heart the thorn that Jesus is offering us. Tomorrow's celebration will be a celebration of tears for us, but I feel that Jesus will be consoled!

. . I would like to say more to you, but words fail me! . . . I was put in charge of writing you in order to console you, but no doubt I have carried out this duty very poorly . . . .Ah! If I were able to convey to you the peace Jesus placed in my soul at the height of my tears, this is what I am asking Him for you who are myself! . . .

(LT 120, Sept 22nd, 1890)

Even though the time appears as a time of sadness, Thérèse knows that she is close to Jesus and so is her father. Her eyes might be dim with tears but she knows God is working his kind purpose in her. She abandons herself to his will which she sees in the events of her life. She has been led by the Spirit away from infantilism to her refuge, Jesus, in whom she finds her life. She sees her life now as a union with the Jesus who was rejected and went to the cross. Her vocation is to pray. In a letter written on August, 1892, she speaks of her insight into the work of prayer.

Dear Céline,

I cannot allow the letter to leave without joining a note to it. For this, I must steal a few moments from Jesus, but He does not hold it against me, for it is about Him that we speak together, without Him no discourse has any charms for our hearts. . . . Céline, the vast solitudes, the enchanting horizons opening up before you must be speaking volumes to your soul? I myself see nothing of all that, but I say with Saint John of the Cross: "My Beloved is the mountains, and lonely, wooded valleys, etc." And this Beloved instructs my soul, He speaks to it in silence, in darkness . . . . Recently, there came a thought to me which I have to tell my Céline. It was one day when I was thinking of what I could do to save souls, a word of the gospel gave me a real light. In days gone by, Jesus said to His disciples when showing them the fields of the ripe corn: "Lift up your eyes and see how the fields are already white enough to be harvested," and a little later: "In truth, the harvest is abundant but the number of labourers is small, ask then the master of the harvest to send labourers." What a mystery! . . . Is not Jesus all-powerful? Are not creatures His who made them? Why, then, does Jesus say: Ask the Lord of the harvest that he send some workers"? Why? . . .Ah! It is because Jesus has so incomprehensible a love for us that He wills that we have a share with Him in the salvation of souls. He wills to do nothing without us. The creator of the universe awaits the prayer of a poor little soul to save other souls redeemed like it at the price of all His Blood. Our own vocation is not to go out to harvest the fields of the ripe corn. Jesus does not say to us: "Lower your eyes, look at the fields and go harvest them." Our mission is still more sublime. These are the words of our Jesus: "Lift up your eyes and see." See how in my heaven there are empty places; it is up to you to fill them, you are my Moses praying on the mountain, ask me for workers, and I shall send them, I await only a prayer, a sigh from your heart! . . .

Is not the apostolate of prayer, so to speak, more elevated than that of the word? Our mission as Carmelites is to form evangelical workers who will save thousands of souls whose mothers we shall be . . . . Céline, if these were not the very words of our Jesus, who would dare to believe in them? . . . I find that our share is really beautiful, what have we to envy in priests? . . . How I would like to be able to tell you all I am thinking, but time is lacking, understand all I could write you! . . .   (LT 135)

Thérèse sees God's wisdom at work (Rom 11:33-36) and in his merciful teaching he uses events to educate us (Heb 12:5-12). He softens the hardened heart (cf Ps 80:13, Rom 1:24, Lk 15:12-13) and this helps our progress to the reality of sharing with Jesus in his work of healing and redemption (see Col 1:24). The heart of Thérèse is Jesus. Without him she would not have faced the life she had. The world in which we live is a world in which we are afraid. We are prisoners of our limitations. We live in a world where darkness, sometimes, seems to have the upper hand. Only God can save us. He came to us in our own condition. He shares our fate to deliver us from it. Jesus emptied himself of all vestiges of power and glory (Phil 2:6-11). As we saw, this is called his 'kenosis', the Greek for his self-emptying. Jesus was wholly unprotected. He experienced the depths of what it meant to be a human being, an unprivileged, poor, helpless man whom the authorities believed could be killed without any consequences. He would, to them, be just one more casualty to the Heart of Darkness. Jesus delivered us from suffering in the sense he gave it meaning. Yet in Jesus' case love conquered death and he calls us to him because he is alive and his Spirit is present among us. To live in union with the life of Jesus is to accept the human heart in all its bitterness as he died, and surrender to the Father in it and through it. On our part we have to come to accept that we are poor, in need and are often helpless. Hidden emotions such as anger and resentment can be deep in our subconscious. We can find ourselves victims of circumstance - such as violence or abuse. We ourselves can be driven by compulsions that we cannot control. We are all wounded. These things teach us our need for Jesus, who brings God and human beings together is our healing and holiness. This is the world Thérèse lived in. There she was in communion with Jesus and prayed, all the time, that others would know the peace of Jesus. Thérèse knew the infinite mercy and love of God. She came to realise that his mercy and love was totally gift. She remained in the presence of God like a child. Picasso, once said that he spent a long time learning to paint like an adult. He said it took him longer before he learned to paint like a child. I see something similar in Thérèse. She left the world of childhood behind, but now she was called to be a spiritual child, welcoming God's love in openness like a little child and radiating that love to others. In the gospel of Mark, when the disciples asked Jesus who is the greatest; "He took a little child whom he set among them and he embraced the child, and he said to them, 'Anyone who welcomes a little child such as this in my name, welcomes me; and anyone who welcomes me, welcomes not me but the one who sent me"   (Mk 9:36f, see also Mt 18:3).

Saint Thérèse offered herself in the trusting, loving attitude of a child to give God pleasure. She wished to forget herself to receive his love and make of her heart a place where his love can expand. His love has been refused by many. Thérèse's great delight was to allow God's love expand in her heart and she prayed this be poured out on others.

The Pathos of God

When we look at the expressions 'console Jesus', 'console God', people say this is anthropomorphic. This means we speak of God in human terms but he is different from us and greater than anything we can say about him. Rabbi Abraham Heschel has given me another perspective. He speaks of the 'Pathos' of God (The Prophets, pp. 247-268). God is concerned for his people and his creation. All the words we use to describe this care and love are inadequate, not because they are wrong, but because God's care and love, his 'pathos', his concern for peace and justice are much greater than we can understand (see The Prophets, pp. 268-279). He, Rabbi Heschel complained that human cruelty and callousness was increasing more and more (The Insecurity of Freedom, p. 37). His call for us was to pray and let God in to cure this darkness. He quotes the prophet Isaiah, "In all their afflictions, he was afflicted" (Is 63:9). He says, "Human is he who is concerned with other selves" (Man is Not Alone, p. 138). He reminds us of the biblical texts "The Lord is near to all who call upon Him, to all who call upon Him in truth" (Ps 145:18) and he also reminds us of what the prophet Hosea said, "For I desire love and not sacrifice, attachment to God rather than burnt offerings" (Ho 6:6). This quotation from Hosea helps us understand Matthew's gospel when Jesus regularly quotes this line from Hosea. The meaning of our existence depends on whether or not we respond to God who is in search of us.

Thérèse and Kenosis

Thérèse would have been familiar with this part of the letter to the Colossians:

He is the image of the unseen God,
the first-born of all creation,
for in him were created all things
in heaven and on earth:
everything visible
and everything invisible,

thrones, ruling forces,
sovereignties, powers -
all things were created through him
and for him.
He exists before all things
and in him all things hold together,
and he is the Head of the Body,
that is, the Church.
He is the Beginning,
the first-born from the dead,
so that he should be supreme in every way
because God wanted all fullness
to be found in him
and through him
to reconcile all things to him,
everything in heaven
and everything on earth,
by making peace through his death
on the cross.

This passage shows the Son's place in God the Father's plan. Thérèse was always touched by the mystery of how this son was incarnate in the humble birth at Bethlehem in poverty and powerlessness. He is the one who freed me and gave himself for me (Gal 2:20). His life announcing the love and mercy of God would lead him to the cross. This was Jesus' self-emptying, kenosis, as described in Phil 2:6-11. Thérèse was very like Francis and Clare, spiritual marriage consists essentially in taking to oneself the littleness and the poverty of Jesus in all the mysteries of his life, from Bethlehem to the cross. One would become little and poor for love of Him.

In her poem 'Jesus, My Beloved, Remember!....' she meditates on the life of Jesus and his need for love.

Remember that your divine Face
Was always unknown to your own people;
But you left your sweet image for me,
And, you know it well, I did recognize you .....
Yes, I know you, all veiled in tears.
Face of the Eternal One, I discover your charms.

Jesus, all the hearts
Who gather your tears,
Remember.

Remember the loving moan
That escaped from your Heart on the cross.
Ah! Jesus, that moan is impressed in my heart,
And I share your burning thirst.
The more I feel myself burning with your divine flames,
The more I thirst to give you souls.
With love's thirst
I burn night and day,
Remember.

Remember, Jesus, Word of Life,
How you loved me and even died for me.
I also want to love you to folly.
I also want to live and die for You.
You know, O my God! All that I desire
Is to make you loved and one day be a martyr.
I want to die of love.
Lord, my desire,
Remember.   (PN 24:24-26)

Thérèse did not want any extraordinary mystical graces. She wanted to live by faith, love and hope. She looked at Mary and her ordinary life in Nazareth. She was one with Mary. She sought Jesus in the 'night of Faith'. We see this in her last poem 'Why I Love You, O Mary!'. She says: "Mother, your sweet Child wants you to be the example of the Soul searching for Him in the night of Faith" (PN 54:15).

When Mary stood at the foot of the cross she had to stand there in faith and abandonment. She had to trust all to the hands of God as she saw her son broken and bruised. This was the fullness of Jesus' kenosis, his total giving of Himself. Mary had to totally give of herself in confidence and trust. This was her kenosis, the kenosis of faith. Mary's yes at the Annunciation led to her yes to God in seeing her son die. This was her share in Jesus' work. John Paul II in his encyclical letter, Redemptoris Mater (Mother of the Redeemer), no. 18, wrote: "on Golgotha . . . (Jesus Christ) was humiliated even more, he was obedient even to death and death on a cross" (Phil 2:5-8). At the foot of the cross, Mary participates by faith in this upsetting sacrifice". He goes on to Mary's part as a kenosis of faith. She has to give all away, all of herself in faith and confidence in God. This is her share in Jesus' saving mission. Mary's heart is a model for Thérèse. Mary is the 'little way'. She had to live a life of poverty, selflessness, confidence and abandonment. Ivan Marcil describes Thérèse's self-giving in her time as her form of kenosis. She travels the way of humility, love and humility as described by St. Paul (Phil 2:1-5), (I. Marcil, p. 456).

Thérèse followed her teacher John of the Cross in not wishing for the extraordinary. She lived a life of faith, "Happy are those who have believed" (Lk 1:45). She remembered the words spoken by Jesus after the resurrection, "Happy are those who believe without having seen" (Jn 20:29). Thérèse had her experiences and she allowed herself to grow in faith. She gave herself in love and poverty. She says in her poem, 'Jesus, My Beloved, Remember!...'

> "Remember that on the day of your victory
> You told us, "He who has not seen
> The Son of God all radiant with glory
> Is blessed if still he has believed!"
> In the shadow of Faith, I love you and adore you.
> O Jesus! I'm waiting in peace for the dawn to see you.
> I don't desire
> To see you here below
>   Remember..."   (PN 24:27)

In Thérèse's last year when she experienced her 'trial of Faith'. She wrote, in DE, "I desired more not to see God and the saints and to rest in the night of faith more than others who desired to see and understand (DE 11.8.5). "I do not desire to see God on this earth. And yet I love him! I love very much the blessed virgin and the saints and I do not wish to see them" (DE 11.9.7). In the first letter of St. Peter we read "You have not seen him, yet you love him; and still without seeing him you believe in him and so are filled with a joy so glorious that it cannot be described and you are sure of the good of your faith, that is, the salvation of your souls (1 Pet 1:8). Thérèse had her faith. It was nurtured by her experiences in childhood and was nourished by the liturgy, her hours spent in prayer before the Blessed Sacrament and by her meditation on sacred scripture. She was guided by the Holy Spirit to understand in her heart the mystery of Jesus and she gave herself in confidence and trust to Jesus. Like Mary at the foot of the cross her dryness in prayer and later her trial of faith did not mean a loss of faith, but it is a faith that faces heroically great distress and trials. Mary who embraced the dead body of her son lived out her trial. Yet she remained faithful. Mary's heart and Thérèse's heart were one in confidence and love, even in the face of great trials. Mary is the little way. Thérèse gave herself more and more for those who felt far from the mercy of God and those who had no faith. She shared with Mary in giving all to Jesus so that all might be saved (1 Tim 2:4).

Thérèse knew the passage from John 14:23f. She quotes it in LT 142 and LT 165. This line reads:

> "Anyone who loves me will keep my word,
> And my Father will love him,
> And we shall come to him
> And make a home in him"   (Jn 14:23)

It is by the power of the Holy Spirit that the trinity indwells in the soul of the person. The Holy Spirit is the Spirit of life who gives life to us. He is also the life of the soul in that he is closer to us than we are to ourselves. He indwells us with the Father and the Son. John of the Cross assures us that our union with God and our transformation by the power of the Holy Spirit is true (Living Flame of Love, Sza. 3). God gives himself generously to the souls that make space for him. Thérèse understood these things with the eyes of faith. She could see that the trinity indwelt in every soul and this helped her love others. She did not need spectacular manifestations of this. She thought of the virgin Mary who lived a life of quiet faith, trusted in God and had a total giving of herself to say yes to God in all things. Mary's heart was the heart of Thérèse - both were imbued with the Holy Spirit.

Chapter Two

'I Will Not Leave You Orphans': The 'Descent to Love'

Eloi Leclerc is a Franciscan friar who lives in France. During the Second World War he and many other friars were made prisoners by the Nazis. The Nazis became afraid of them and sent the friars and many other 'undesirables' to Dachau. Many died. Eloi describes the horror of the experience in his work "The Canticle of Creatures" (pp. 227-236). He describes how God seemed to be silent and absent. He felt abandoned. He saw many people die alone and with no comfort, no hope. While they were packed into a wagon on the way to Dachau one of his friends, a fellow friar, was dying. Eloi and the others had been tortured and were suffering from hunger and thirst and disease. However his dying friend had one last gift for the others before he died. Instead of thinking of himself, he thought of the others and the pain they were in. He began to sing St. Francis' 'Canticle of the Creatures'. He died singing this in the arms of Eloi and the others. They felt courage return - a light had shone in their darkness. They felt that they were not alone. God was there in their suffering.

Jesus had promised: "I will not leave you orphans" (Jn 14:18). He said:

> "I shall ask the Father
> and he will give you another Paraclete
> to be with you forever,
> the Spirit of truth whom the world can never accept
> since it neither sees nor knows him;
> but you know him,
> because he is with you, he is in you"   (Jn 14:15-17)

Eloi, after his release by the allies began to rethink his faith. He looked at Jesus, the poor crucified one. In his book "Le Royaume Caché" (The Hidden Kingdom) he meditates on the life of the poor Jesus. It is interesting that he uses the word 'hidden', a word Thérèse used often. He shows how love overcame death and we are called to new life in Jesus' spirit.

Yet in the epilogue of the book, "Le Silence de l'aube" (The Silence of the Dawn), pp. 217-224, he argues that we are only at the dawn of this new age.

He alludes again to the lonely death of so many in the camps. In the modern world in which we live many still die lonely and without hope. There are few to bring the Spirit of new life to them. For me his life and work echo St. Thérèse's hope for 'little souls' to join her to bring light to those in darkness. As we will see, Thérèse articulated the 'little way' as a gift of the Holy Spirit to all. We are not called to imitate her. She lived the 'little way' more and more heroically as the years went on, especially in her 'trial of faith' of the last eighteen months of her life. She is the great teacher, but we, her students, as it were, are called to live the way as best we can. The friend of Eloi Leclerc who died on the train with his dying breath he gave courage and life to those around him. We can be lights in the darkness for those who suffer in our world. This is the essence of the 'little way' for me.

Thérèse on the Way to Union:

Thérèse tells us of her days in Carmel that spiritual aridity was her daily bread (MsA, 73v°). Her guide in prayer was John of the Cross. "At the age of seventeen and eighteen I had no other spiritual nourishment (MsA, 83r°). She adds that Holy Scripture and her memory of the Imitation were also her nourishment. From John of the Cross she learnt that God worked in dryness and 'apparent' absence. She had an obstinate streak and she continued to pray in aridity and without consolation. She abandoned all to God's 'hidden' work in her.

In a letter to Céline in the summer of 1893 (LT 142), Thérèse wrote the following ". . .it is Jesus who does all and I do nothing." In MsC, 12v°, she says: "The more I am united to Him (Jesus), the more I love my sisters." St. Paul wrote in the letter to the Galatians: "In part through the law I am dead to the law so that I can be alive to God. I have been crucified with Christ and yet I am alive; yet it is no longer I but Christ living in me. The life I am now living, subject to the limitations of human nature, I am living in faith, faith in the Son of God who loved me and gave himself for me (Gal 2:19-20). Thérèse made these words her own. She was one with Jesus in his self-giving and she knew he loved her. Her prayer was 'dryness' but she lived in faith like St. Paul. She made real again in her life what Paul had said of his. Thérèse used this text from St. Paul in MsA, 36r°, LT 184. She quotes this passage in poem 17, "Vivre d'Amour" (To Live for Love).

> "Living on love is living on your life,
> Glorious King, delight of the elect."   (PN13, 3)

And from poem 24, "Jesus my Beloved, Remember!"

"O Bread of the exiled Holy and divine Host
It is no longer I who live, but I live on your life."
(PN24, 29)

Hans Urs Von Balthazar (1905-1988) was a theologian who argued that the rift between dogmatic thinking and spirituality be healed and that the work and life of the mystics teach us about Jesus' heart and makes Jesus present in a new generation. He says of the mystics:

"Their charism consisted in their ability to
re-immerse themselves beyond everything that convention
might dictate, in a 'contemporaneity' with
the gospel so as to bequeath the legacy
of their intimate experience to their spiritual children."
(Von Balthasar, Mysterium Paschale, p. 38)

Jesus is alive and by the power of the Holy Spirit is ever present and active. Von Balthasar sees 'contemporaneity with the gospel' as a participation of the believer in the eternal aspect of the definitive, historical saving events of Jesus. The saints are the ones who hear God's call and respond. Thérèse came to know Jesus and now by the work of the Holy Spirit, she was being transformed so that she could say with Paul "it is no longer I but Christ living in me" (Gal 2:20). As Von Balthasar said she was one of the mystics who made real the living word of God in her life, prayer and influence. Jesus said: "As the Father has loved me, so I have loved you" (Jn 15:9).

This was the Jesus Thérèse has come to know. He was still alive and he was her inner teacher. The Jesus of love and mercy was the one who helped Thérèse interpret scripture and her life. John of the Cross showed how Jesus acted in the soul by the power of the Holy Spirit. This was especially true when prayer appeared to be dry and without consolation and Jesus appeared to be silent. Yet with confidence and love Thérèse knew he was working his kind purposes on her.

Thérèse and Zacchaeus (Lk 19:5)

The Gospel of John tells us of Jesus: "He came to his own people and his own people did not accept him" (Jn 1:11). He was brought to death by these people but to "all who did accept him, he gave power to become children of God" (Jn 1:12). Jesus prays for those who are his own. He says:

"May they all be one,
just as, Father, you are in me
and I am in you,
so that they also may be in us,
so that the world may believe
it was you who sent me
I have given them the glory,
you gave to me,
that they may be one as we are one"   (Jn 17:22-23)

Thérèse gave herself over to God by working away upon all her acting, willing, thinking, so that in everything, in every little way, she may "embody the Word of Love in her life" (Von Balthasar, Thérèse of Lisieux, p.16f). Thérèse's new Christ-self is precisely the self she so self-consciously fashions from the daily details of her life.

On 10th May, 1892, after three years in the Asylum du Bon-Saveur in Caen, Monsieur Martin returned to Lisieux. The next day uncle Guerin brought Louis to see his daughters in Carmel. He was very ill and in a wheelchair. He pointed upwards and said "an ciel" (in Heaven). There they would find peace (see the testimony of Mother Agnes in Histoire d'une Ame, SS, 1898, pp. 136-137, also CGII, p. 662). As Thérèse watched the last days of her father, she recognised that he had a special communion with the suffering servant vocation of Jesus and God was working through his darkness.

Céline wrote a letter to Madame La Néele, her first cousin, in which she describes the state of Louis. She speaks of his days of infinite sorrow, his many tears. Céline feels his pain. She writes: "Yesterday he said to me, 'kindly pray for me'" (25 July, 1892, CGII, p. 662).

At this time Thérèse's spiritual life was nourished more and more by sacred scripture, especially the gospels "I am always discovering new lights in them, meanings hidden and mysterious" (MsA, 83v°). Céline was the first to receive parts of this prayer.

She wrote to Céline on 19th October and she quotes the gospel concerning the visit of Jesus to Zacchaeus (Lk 19:1-10). She tells Céline "Like Zacchaeus, we climbed a tree to see Jesus. . ." (Lk 19:4). Later she says:

"... Céline, what a mystery is our grandeur in Jesus. . . . This is all that Jesus has shown us in making us climb the symbolic tree about which I was just talking to you. And now what science is He about to teach us? Has He not taught us all? . . . Let us listen to what He is saying to us: "Make haste to descend, I must lodge today at your house." Well, Jesus tells us to descend. . . . Where, then, must we descend? Céline, you know better than I, however, let me tell you where we must now follow Jesus. In days gone by, the Jews asked our divine Saviour: "Master, where do you live?" And He answered: "The foxes have their lairs, the birds of heaven their nests, but I have no place to rest my head." This is where we must descend in order that we may serve as an abode for Jesus. To be so poor that we do not have a place to rest our head." This is, dear Céline, what Jesus has done in my soul during my retreat. . . . You understand, there is question here of the interior. Besides, has not the exterior already been reduced to nothing by means of the very sad trial of Caen? . . . In our dear Father, Jesus has stricken us in the most sensitive exterior part of our heart; now let us allow Him to act, He can complete His work in our souls . . . What Jesus desires is that we receive Him into our hearts. No doubt, they are already empty of creatures, but, alas, I feel mine is not entirely empty of myself, and it is for this reason that Jesus tells me to descend . . . He, the King of kings, humbled Himself in such a way that His face was hidden, and no one recognised Him. . . And I, too, want to hide my face, I want my Beloved alone to see it, that He be the only one to count my tears. . That in my heart at least He may rest His dear head and feel that there He is known and understood!. . .

Céline, I cannot tell you all I would like, my soul is powerless. . . Ah, if only I could!. . . But, no, this is not in my power . . . Why be sad, do you not always think what I am thinking? . . . Thus all I do not tell you, you divine. Jesus makes you feel it in your heart. Has He not, moreover, set up His abode there to console Himself for the crimes of sinners? Yes, it is there in the intimate retreat of the soul that He instructs us together, and one day He will show us the day which will no longer have any setting . . . (LT, 137)

The way of Thérèse is to welcome Jesus and God's will into their hearts, accepting the present moment of loneliness and offering it to God so that through their sufferings the world may be healed, the darkness overcome. In this way "Jesus is consoled." She is powerless to do anything except to allow the Spirit of Love to enter her soul, so that this love can be poured on others. Jesus' call is a call of love to Zacchaeus. He must stay in Zacchaeus' house (Lk 19:5) and Thérèse makes this call her own. Jesus had told Zacchaeus that he had come "to save that which was lost" (Lk 19:9). In the suffering face of her father she saw the suffering face of Jesus and realised that it is our union with Jesus in his abandonment that one achieves God's will. Jesus had said "My food is to do the will of my Father" (Jn 4:34). Thérèse knew she had to give herself unconditionally to Jesus' love and the mysterious way it worked. She was on the road to confidence and trust in the Other who is God.

In the letter 137, she encouraged Céline to come down from the 'tree' of her own securities and humbly give herself to God and place her trust in him.

At the end of 1892 Thérèse had to battle and master the family trial. Around this time, again, the old disease of scruples began to surface again. Fr. Pichon wrote to her assuring her she had never committed a mortal sin (LC 151, 20 Jan 1893). Fr. Pichon had already assured this in May 1888 (see MsA, 70r°). These reassurances helped Thérèse win another battle. In the 'Final Conversations', she places Fr. Pichon alongside Fr. Prou in doing a lot of good to her soul (DE, 4.7.4). Dr. Robert Masson said that Thérèse had an inner wound which required continual healing. He argued that the wound persisted even to her death (see R. Masson, Souffrance des hommes, p. 69). Pierre-Jean Thomas-Lamotte is another doctor who looked at the wound of Thérèse. He points out that the spiritual person grows from the psychic-human person. He locates Thérèse's wound, her fear of abandonment, in her early days when she had to be sent to a wet nurse. Then came the shock of Zélie's death and later there was Pauline's entry into Carmel. All of these made Thérèse a wounded person. As she grew in the life of the Spirit she was being internally cured over a period of time - the grace of Christmas, the release of the excess of scruples, Fr. Prou's launching of her on the way of confidence and love and Fr. Pichon's repeated reassurances (see P-J Thomas Lamotte, Guérir Avec Thérèse).

Through all these people and events God was healing Thérèse of her inner woundedness. With each healing her confidence in God's loving kindness and mercy grew and she surrendered herself more and more into his hands. She gives herself to God's will. "She embraces the sacrifice God asks of her" (Von Balthasar, Thérèse of Lisieux, p. 234f). She is on her way to incarnating "love in the heart of the Church" (MsB, 3r°). She has not yet reached this 'eureka' moment. A new Thérèse and a new vibrant Thérèse is coming to life. A new reality of God's love comes to be incarnate in her in the world by means of her self-giving. Jesus said in John's gospel: "I loved you just as the Father loved me. Remain in my love" (Jn 15:9) and then he says: "This is my commandment. Love one another as I have loved you" (Jn 15:12). This describes the new Thérèse.

Another date is important at this time. Mother Agnes (Pauline) was elected prioress. Thérèse describes her joy on the election of Pauline, she became her mother once more: "On that day Pauline became my living Jesus" (MsA, 80v°). She also wrote a letter to Mother Agnes 20th Feb, 1893 saying the following:

Dear Mother,

How sweet it is for me to be able to give you this name! . . . For a long time already you were my Mother, but it was in the secret of my heart I was giving this sweet name to her who was at once my guardian Angel and my Sister. Today God has consecrated you. . . . Oh! How beautiful this day is for your child! . . . The veil Jesus has cast over this day makes it more luminous in my eyes, it is the seal of the Adorable Face, the perfume of the mysterious bouquet that is poured out on you. No doubt, this will always be the same. "He whose face was hidden," He who is still hidden in His little white Host and who communicates Himself to souls only as veiled, will be able to spread upon the entire life of the beloved apostle of His divine Face a mysterious veil which He alone can penetrate!. . .

Yes, Mother Geneviève's spirit lives entirely in you, and her prophetic word has been realised. At thirty you have begun your public life. Is it not you who gave to all the Carmels and to so many pious souls the consolation of the touching and poetic account of our Saint's life? . . . But already Jesus had cast on my dear Mother His veiled look, and He did not allow her to be recognised, for her face was hidden!. . .   (LT, 140)

We get a pen picture of Thérèse around this time from Sr. Marie of the Angels. She describes Thérèse:

Sr. Thérèse of The Child Jesus, twenty years old. Novice and jewel of the Carmel, its dear Benjamin. Office of painting in which she excels without having had any other lessons than those of seeing our Reverend Mother, her dear sister, at work. Tall and strong, with the appearance of a child, a tone of voice, an expression, hiding within her a wisdom, a perfection, a perspicacity of a fifty-year-old. Soul always calm and in perfect possession of itself in all things and with everybody. Little innocent thing, to whom one would give God without confession, but whose head is full of mischief to play on anyone she pleases. Mystic, comic, everything. . . She can make you weep with devotion and just as easily split your sides with laughter during our recreations." (To the Visitation at Le Mans, 1893.)

The former prioress, Mother Marie de Gonzague, was named mistress of novices, and Sister Marie of the Angels was elected sub prioress. Oldest in the novitiate, Thérèse was invited by Mother Agnes "to watch over her two companions, Sister Martha and Sister Marie-Madeleine" (NPPAO, Virtue of Prudence). Mother Marie de Gonzague agreed "to be aided by her in correcting and occasionally instructing them" (ibid.). There was nothing new in this regarding Sister Martha. As for Sister Marie-Madeleine, Thérèse never succeeded in winning over this gloomy companion, marked by an unhappy childhood.

She was a person of great fear. She tried to avoid Thérèse where she could - even leaving spiders (which Thérèse hated) in her path so that she would not follow her. Thérèse knew she had been badly hurt as a child, so she resolved to be even more kind in looking after her.

Céline, now twenty-four years old, was going through a complicated crisis. In spite of her filial tenderness - we should call it: maternal - for her sick father, it was difficult for her to be unable to realize her vocation. Léonie left her in order to enter the Visitation once more: Marie Guérin made her decision to enter Carmel. Céline felt that she had been cast aside, a family stray. Moreover, P. Pichon had placed her in a compromising situation regarding her sisters, asking her to keep secret his plan for a religious foundation in Canada.

Agnes asked Thérèse to help Celine by writing regularly to her. Thérèse guided her gently and in her letters we begin to see the first proper articulation of the 'Little Way'.

Léonie was called by Thérèse, "poor little Léonie". Once when I was writing this work I made a list of Thérèse's sisters and suddenly I realised I had forgotten Léonie! Once again, "poor little Léonie." She had a difficult temperament and could be full of anxiety and depression. Her attempt to join the Visitation nuns at Caen in 1893 was her second attempt at a religious vocation, but she left the convent in 1895. Thérèse never ceased praying for her, believing one day she would succeed. Léonie entered the convent of the Visitation in 1899. This time she succeeded and took the name Sister Françoise-Thérèse. She died in 1941. Today there is a steady trickle of people to Léonie's graveside. They draw comfort from her struggles and her prayers. Those who suffer from hidden fears, anxiety, nervous illnesses and depression find solace from Léonie and entrusting themselves to her prayers. "Poor Little Léonie" made it in the end. Thérèse knew this and always had faith in Léonie.

The Drops of Dew that Sparkle (LT 141) (April 25, 1893)

The image of a flower is one that Thérèse used often. She describes Manuscript A as the 'Springtime story of a little flower written by herself and dedicated to Reverend Mother Agnes of Jesus" (MsA, 2r°) and in this work she says: "I shall begin to sing what I must sing eternally: 'The Mercies of the Lord' (Ps 88:2)" (MsA, 2r°). In MsA she uses the image of the flower to refer to herself more than 30 times. She calls herself the 'little flower of Jesus' (MsA, 3v°, 26v°, 31v°), 'the little flower of the good God' (MsA, 13r°, 50v°) and 'the little flower of the Virgin Mary' (MsA, 27v°, 30v°, 35v°, 40r°, 77r°, 85v°).

Thérèse wrote to Céline for Céline's twenty-fourth birthday. Thérèse wrote this letter two months after she had written her first poem, 'The Divine Dew' (PN 1) in which she used the image of the flower and the dewfall. The divine dew is the virginal milk of Mary. She says:

My Sweet Jesus, You appear to me
On your Mother's breast, all radiant with love.
Love is the ineffable mystery
That exiled you from your Heavenly Home. . .
Ah! Let me hide myself under the veil
Concealing you from all mortal eyes,
And near you, O Morning Star!
I shall find a foretaste of Heaven. (PN 1,1)

Donald Kinney, O.C.D, in his introduction to this poem says the following:

> There is no denying that it has real naïve beauty. Behind Thérèse's inexperience, especially in the continuity and adaptation of her images, we see true poetic gifts revealed: an ability to create access to "more hidden mysteries of a superior order" through images (GCII, p. 748). Already in this attempt we find a whole Thérèsian thematic: the flower, blood, the rose, and dew (In French, note the play on words: la rose - the rose - and la rosée - dew), the seraphim, love, the brotherhood of Jesus, the Eucharist, etc. (The Poetry of Saint Thérèse, p. 37).

Thérèse develops the theme of the flower and the dew in her letter to Céline. The poem expressed the love of Mary for Jesus, her son. Here the letter expresses the love of bride and bridegroom. The flower, love, symbolises Jesus in all the mysteries of his earthly life, from the incarnation to the Cross. The dew in the letter symbolises the total giving of the bride to the bridegroom who thirsts for love. Thérèse uses the expression: "Jesus alone" (PN 2).

In both the poem and the letter the symbol of the flower symbolises the 'littleness' of Jesus. Thérèse was very influences by the self-emptying, the kenosis of Jesus (see Phil 2:6-11). He took the form of a slave (Phil 2:6). As Jesus grew he became painfully familiar with the alienation from God in which others live. He entered this world of pain to heal the break between human beings and God. This would cost his life, but by the power of God he overcame death and opened the door for reconciliation with God. Jesus said 'where I am, there must my servant be also' (Jn 12:26). Thérèse was one of the servants Jesus called and Thérèse hopes to encourage Celine to be one also. Also Jesus became a little one, so Thérèse must become little so as to have a place in his heart.

The letter is spontaneous. Thérèse describes how she was praying before the Blessed Sacrament and she was praying for Céline. For Thérèse, as was the case for Francis and Clare, 'spiritual marriage' consists essentially in taking to oneself the littleness and the poverty of Jesus in all the life-giving mysteries of his life, from his birth to the Cross, all the time making oneself as a little poor one for love of Him.

The parable of the flower and the dew are re-interpreted here in the symbol of marriage. Thérèse uses the Canticle of Canticles to show her point. The 'canticle' is made up of love poetry that accompany a marriage. She quotes the following: "I am the rose of Sharon, the lily of the valleys" (Ct 2:1). The bridegroom, Jesus, is the same one who asks the Samaritan woman for a drink of water (Jn 4:7). For Thérèse the flower is thirsty, but is so small that all it needs is a tiny drop of dew. The bride must become so little that she becomes the dewfall for the little flower.

The symbol of the embrace of love, to be in his arms, appears at the end of LT 143, Thérèse says: "I abandon myself into the arms of Jesus. The little drop of dew goes deeper into the calyx of the flower of the fields, and there it finds all it has lost and even much more" (LT 143). The word 'abandon' is now entering Thérèse's vocabulary. Thérèse sees the heart of Jesus in all its corporeal reality. At the time of Thérèse the wound in the side of Jesus becomes the wound of the heart. The blood and water that flow from the heart symbolises the outpouring of love and life in the Spirit that Jesus' life-giving death brings (see Jn 19:31-37). Thérèse loved the image of the Sacred Heart. She unites herself with the Heart of her beloved. In her poem, "To the Sacred Heart of Jesus" (PN 23) she expresses her wish not just to 'rest on the Sacred Heart of Jesus' (Sza.5) but to 'hide herself' in the Sacred Heart (Sza.7). In the last verse Thérèse describes how she would like to enter Heaven:

> To be able to gaze on your glory,
> I know we have to pass through fire.
> So I, for my purgatory,
> Choose your burning love, O heart of my God!
> On leaving this life, my exiled soul
> Would like to make an act of pure love,
> And then, flying away to Heaven, its Homeland,
> Enter straightaway into your Heart.
>
> (PN 23, 8)

Here we see Thérèse's talk of the act of pure love. She was influenced by St. John of the Cross who said: "The smallest movement of pure love is more useful to the church than all other works put together . . . . Thus, it is of greatest importance that our souls be exercised much in Love so that being consumed quickly we do not linger here on earth but soon attain the vision of Jesus, Face to Face". This is taken from the "Spiritual Canticle" 13, commentary on Sza.29. We see here the words of her discovery in 1896: "My vocation is love" (MsB, 2r°). In her last conversations she says:

"With what longing and what consolation I repeated from the beginning of my religious life these other words of St. John of the Cross: 'It is of the highest importance that the soul practice love very much in order that, being consumed rapidly, she may be scarcely retained here on earth but promptly reach the vision of her God face to face'"

(DE 7.27.5).

At the end of August, another statement that is crucial to our subject:

"Ah! It is incredible how all my hopes have been fulfilled. When I used to read St. John of the Cross, I begged God to work out in me what he wrote, that is, the same thing as though I were to live to be very old; to consume me rapidly in Love, and I have been answered!" (DE 8.31.9).

She also quotes this part of St. John of the Cross in a letter she wrote to Roulland, a missionary in China (LT 221). Thérèse begins her letter to Céline with the thoughts that struck her as she prayed before the Tabernacle:

I am going to tell you a thought that came to me this morning, or rather I am going to share with you the desires of Jesus concerning your soul . . . . When I think of you in the presence of the one friend of our souls, it is always simplicity that is presented to me as the distinctive characteristic of your heart . . . . Céline! . . . simple little Céline-flower, do not envy garden flowers. Jesus has not said to us: "I am the flower of the fields and the Lily of the valleys." Well, I thought this morning near the Tabernacle, that my Céline, the little flower of Jesus, had to be and to remain always a drop of dew hidden in the divine corolla of the beautiful Lily of the valleys. A drop of dew, what is more simple and more pure? It is not the clouds that have formed it since, when the blue of the sky is star-studded, the dew descends on the flowers; it is not comparable to the rain that it surpasses in freshness and beauty. Dew exists only at night; as soon as the sun darts its warm rays, it distils the charming pearls that sparkle on the tips of blades of grass in the meadow, and the dew is changed into a light vapour. Céline is a little drop of dew that has not been formed by the clouds but has descended from the beautiful heaven, its homeland.

Here Thérèse sees the Carmelite vocation in the light of the kenosis of Jesus. It is a sharing in his becoming 'lonely' and all the time surrendering himself to God's will. Céline experienced a time of dryness and sadness. Thérèse uses the image of a 'drop of dew' to show that Céline's heart is hidden in God. Thérèse sees the Carmelite vocation as one of quiet, hidden self-giving. Thérèse goes on to develop the image of the flower and the dew:

During the night of life, its mission is to hide itself in the heart of the Flower of the fields; no human eye is to discover it there, only the calyx possessing the little drop will know its freshness. Blessed little drop of dew that is only known by Jesus! . . . Do not stop to consider the course of resounding rivers that cause admiration in creatures. Do not even envy the clear brook winding in the meadow. No doubt its murmur is very sweet, but creatures can hear it . . . And then the calyx of the flower of the fields would be unable to contain it. It could not be for Jesus alone. To be His, one must remain little, little like a drop of dew! . . . Oh! How few are the souls who aspire to remain little in this way! . . . "But," they say, "are not the river and the brook more useful than the drop of dew, what does it do? It is good for nothing except to refresh for a few moments a flower of the fields which is today and will have disappeared tomorrow." . . . Undoubtedly these persons are right, the drop of dew is good only for that; but they do not know the wild flower that willed to live on our earth of exile and to remain there during the short night of life. If they did know it, they would understand the reproach that Jesus made in the days gone by to Martha . . . Our Beloved has no need of our beautiful thoughts and our dazzling works. If He wants sublime thoughts, does He not have His angels, His legions of heavenly spirits whose knowledge infinitely surpasses that of the greatest geniuses of our sad earth? . . . It is not, then, intelligence and talents that Jesus has come to seek here below. He became the flower of the fields only in order to show us how much He cherishes simplicity. The Lily of the valley longs only for a little drop of dew . . . . And it is for this reason He has created one whose name is Céline! . . . During the night of life, she will have to remain hidden from every human glance, but when the shadows begin to lengthen, when the Flower of the fields becomes the Sun of Justice, and when He comes to carry out His giant's race, will He forget His little drop of dew? . . .

Here Thérèse describes what she means by little. It is the humble, gentle one who gives love, like a little child. One must not be full of oneself but generous and self-giving. Thérèse becomes poor, giving all away. She makes herself small, tiny like a drop of dew, so that she can give all to Jesus, everything to Him and Him alone.

The expression 'during the night of life' is repeated three times here. This characterises the life on earth of Jesus and his bride. Thérèse shows that the life of Jesus is real for her in her time and for us today. There is a contemporaneity between her and the gospels to use Von Balthasar's term. She wishes to share in his self giving, his kenosis, when he was poor and gave himself for the love of all. Here Thérèse is very close to the privilege of poverty of Francis and Clare. Francis and Clare saw in Jesus' poverty his humble love. God was so generous in Jesus that he gave away everything so that we may have life. Thérèse saw that Jesus thirsted for love and this was her vocation. She would give herself away to bring Jesus love and to allow his love to radiate through her on those she would care for and pray for. She unites herself to the loving heart of Jesus. This helps us understand the language of marriage that she uses. She saw herself and Céline sharing in Jesus' life on earth and making the saving power of this life present in their lives. The way Thérèse has chosen is to imitate the kenosis of the Word made flesh and give of herself totally. She surrenders all in confidence to him. Thérèse had referred in LT 108, 1890, to the suffering servant and this helps her in understanding the 'hiddeness' of Jesus and how she will remain hidden in him. In this way she will allow the Spirit to act in her. Letter 141 shows how she wishes to live for Jesus alone. She is united with Jesus and Him crucified.

In her poem "Living on Love! . . ." (Vivre d'Amour), PN 17 Thérèse speaks of Mary of Bethany (who she mixes up with Mary Magdalene):

Living on Love is imitating Mary,
Bathing your divine feet that she kisses, transported.
With tears, with precious perfume,
She dries them with her long hair. . .
Then standing up, she shatter the vase,
And in turn she anoints your Sweet Face.
As for me, the perfume with which I anoint your Face
    Is my Love! . . .

"Living on Love, what strange folly!"
The world says to me, "Ah! Stop your singing,
Don't waste your perfumes, your life.
Learn to use them well . . ."
Loving you, Jesus, is such a fruitful loss! . . .
All my perfumes are yours forever.
I want to sing on leaving this world:
    "I'm dying of Love!"   (PN 17, 12-13)

Jesus is thirsty for love. Mary gives him an act of love in washing his feet. Thérèse is teaching us that we can give him love in the Spirit and live our lives from that place. Thérèse said "We experience such great peace when we're totally poor, when we depend on no-one except God" (DE, 8.6.4). She would also, say: "O Jesus, I know it, love is repaid by love alone" (MsB, 4r°). This expression is inspired by the Canticle where John says "the wounds of love are healed only by love" (Spiritual Canticle, Sza.9). In this communion of love, the soul loving Jesus and Jesus loving the soul, pure love is present. This gift of pure love is a gift of the Holy Spirit. The Holy Spirit consubstantial love between God the Father and the Son. Thérèse writes in her poem "Living for Love! . . .", (PN 17) of the Spirit of love:

The spirit of Love sets me aflame with his fire.
In loving you I attract the Father.
My weak heart holds him forever
O Trinity! You are Prisoner
    Of my Love! . . .   (PN 17.2)

Thérèse, in MsA, was thinking of the time she spent with Céline. She was meditating on the words of the Canticle:

Following Your footprints
Maidens run lightly along the way;
The touch of a spark,
The special wine,
Cause flowings in them from the balsam of God.

She thinks of herself and Céline as they prayed together. She says:

"Yes, it was very lightly we followed in Jesus' footprints. The sparks of love He sowed so generously in our souls, and the delicious and strong wine He gave us to drink made all passing things disappear before our eyes, and from our lips came aspirations of love inspired only by Him"

(MsA, 47v°/48r°).

In Living on Love Thérèse evokes this lightness due to love:

Living on Love is giving without limit
Without claiming any wages here below.
Ah! I give without counting, truly sure
That when one loves, one does not keep count! . . .
Overflowing with tenderness, I have given everything,
To his Divine Heart . . . Lightly I run.
I have nothing left by my only wealth:
Living on Love   (PN 17.5)

The Grace of Abandon (LT 142, July 6th, 1893)

This is the first time Thérèse will use the word 'abandon'. It shows the emergence of the 'little way' of spiritual childhood as she gives all as a child to God the Father. The letter looks at how to let Jesus do all in her. Thérèse says, quoting Is 55:8, "My thoughts are not your thoughts". Merit does not consist in doing, or giving much, but rather in receiving, in loving much . . ." when Jesus wills to take for himself the sweetness of giving, it would not be gracious to refuse." That which is important is to allow Jesus to give or take as he pleases; "perfection consists in doing his will", it means doing his will not our own.

The nub of this quest is as Thérèse says to Céline: "What she must do is abandon herself, surrender herself, without keeping anything, . . ." Jesus is teaching Thérèse to play at the bank of love". She confesses she is not in the heights but Jesus is teaching her how to draw profit from the good and the bad she finds in herself. She learns to love not looking at herself or her weaknesses but Jesus Himself.

Our Lord wills me to leave the faithful sheep in the desert. How much this says to me! . . . He is sure to them; they could no longer go astray, for they are captives of love. So Jesus takes away His tangible presence from them in order to give His consolations to sinners. If He does lead them to Tabor, it is for a few moments, the valley is most frequently the place of His repose. "It is there He takes his rest at midday." The morning of our life has passed, we have enjoyed the perfumed breezes of the dawn. Then everything smiled at us, Jesus was making us feel His sweet presence, but when the sun became hot, the Beloved led us into His garden, He made us gather the myrrh of trial by separating us from everything and from Himself. The hill of myrrh has strengthened us with its bitter scents, so Jesus has made us come down again, and now we are in the valley. He leads us beside the waters. . . . Dear Céline, I do not know too well what I am saying to you, but it seems you will understand, divine what I would like to say. Ah! Let us be always Jesus' drop of dew. In that is happiness, perfection . . . Fortunately, I am speaking to you, for other persons would be unable to understand my language.

Thérèse knows she is beginning to use a new language. Her director is Jesus by the power of the Holy Spirit. It is he who teaches her to do for love, to refuse him nothing and he teaches her to be thankful when she is given an opportunity to prove she loves him. In MsB, 4r° she says: "Well, the little child (Thérèse) will strew flowers, she will perfume the royal throne with their sweet scents, and she will sing in silvery tones the canticle of love (MsB, 4r°) Thérèse is a child of God who cures his thirst for love by love.

Céline had written to Thérèse about the illness of Louis and the departure of Léonie for the convent in Caen (LD, 3 July 1893). This allows Thérèse to speak to her of surrendering to Jesus, of letting Him take care of her and to allow Him to place her where he wills. Thérèse writes:

In fact, directors have others advance in perfection by having them perform a great number of acts of virtue, and they are right; but my director, who is Jesus, teaches me not to count up my acts. He teaches me to do all through love, to refuse Him nothing, to be content when He gives me a chance of proving to Him that I love Him. But this is done in peace, in abandonment, it is Jesus who is doing all in me, and I am doing nothing.

The secret is to give all to Jesus in abandonment and allow Him to work. This is an act of pure love. Thérèse feels very close to Céline in her night of suffering. She goes on to say:

I feel very much united to my Céline. I believe God has not often made two souls who understand each other so well, never a discordant note. The hand of Jesus touching one of the lyres makes the other vibrate at the same time . . . . Oh! Let us remain hidden in our divine Flower of the fields until the shadows lengthen; let us allow the drops of liqueur to be appreciated by creatures. Since we are pleasing our Lily, let us remain joyfully His drop, His single drop of dew! . . . And to this drop that has consoled Him during the exile, what will He not give us in the homeland? . . . He tells us Himself: "He who is thirsty, let him come to me and drink," and so Jesus is and will be our ocean . . . . Like the thirsty hind we long for this water that is promised to us, but our consolation is great: to be the ocean of Jesus also, the ocean of the Lily of the valleys! . . .

Your heart alone will be able to read this letter, for I myself have difficulty in deciphering it. I have no more ink, I was obliged to spit into our inkwell to make some . . . Is this not something to laugh about? . . .

I kiss the whole family, but especially my dear king, who will receive a kiss from my Céline from his queen.

Sister Thérèse of The Child Jesus of the Holy Face

Jesus has poured himself out in love. This is his kenosis. Thérèse's insight is that this love is not loved and is thirsty for love. She gives herself in love to Jesus and this a communion between them in the Holy Spirit. This allows Jesus' love to be poured out on others. Thérèse's insight is that we must trust Jesus like children trust and surrender into his arms. For Céline the times are sad, but Thérèse has learnt over the years to surrender all into the hands of God and allow Him to work. That is what she now shares with Céline. Abandonment ('abandon' in French) is now part and parcel of Thérèse's life. In the next two letters LT 143, 144 Thérèse encourages Céline to persevere in this way during the times she feels alone and dry without comfort.

Hidden Life in Jesus (LT 145, August 2nd, 1893)

Here Thérèse meditates on the silence of Jesus, in 'hidden' presence. He has become poor so that we might be able to love him. He is at our mercy - we can refuse to love. Thérèse says:

Your letter filled me with consolation. The road on which you are walking is a royal road, it is not a beaten track, but a path traced out by Jesus Himself. The spouse of the Canticles says that, not having found her Beloved in her bed, she arose to look for Him in the city but in vain; after having gone out of the city, she found Him whom her soul loved! . . . Jesus does not will that we find His adorable presence in repose; He hides Himself; He wraps Himself in darkness. It was not thus that He acted with the crowd of Jews, for we see in the gospel that the people were CARRIED AWAY when He was speaking. Jesus used to charm weak souls with His divine words, He was trying to make them strong for the day of trial . . . But how small was the number of Our Lord's friends when He was SILENT before His judges! . . . Oh! What a melody for my heart in this silence of Jesus. . . . He made Himself poor that we might be able to give Him love. He holds out His hand to us like a beggar so that on the radiant day of judgement when the He will appear in His glory, He may have us hear those sweet words: "Come, blessed of my Father, for I was hungry and you gave me to eat; I was thirsty, and you gave me to drink; I did not know where to lodge, and you gave me a home. I was in prison, sick, and you helped me." It is Jesus Himself who spoke these words; it is He who wants our love, who begs for it . . . He places Himself, so to speak, at our mercy, He does not want to take anything unless we give it to Him, and the smallest thing is precious in His divine eyes. . .

Thérèse calls Jesus a beggar for our love. In St. Francis' prayer, the Absorbeat, he speaks of Jesus "who died for love of my love." She goes on to:

Jesus is a hidden treasure, an inestimable good which few souls can find, for it is hidden, and the world loves what sparkles. Ah! If Jesus had willed to show Himself to all souls with His ineffable gifts, no doubt there is not one of them that would have despised Him. However, He does not will that we love Him for His gifts, He Himself must be our reward. To find a hidden thing one must hide oneself; our life must then be a mystery. We must be like Jesus, Jesus whose face was hidden. . . . "Do you want to learn something that may be of use to you?" says the Imitation. 'love to be unknown and accounted for nothing . . . . And elsewhere; "After you have left everything, you must above all leave yourself; let one man boast of one thing, another of something else; as for you, place your joy only in contempt of yourself." What peace these words give to the soul, Céline. You know them, but do you not know all I would like to say to you? . . . Jesus loves you with a love so great that, if you were to see it, you would be in an ecstasy of happiness that would cause your death, but you do not see it, and you are suffering.

Soon Jesus will stand up to save all the meek and humble of the earth! . . .

Here Thérèse uses scriptural quotations along with pieces from the Imitation of Christ and the 'Spiritual Canticle' of John of the Cross (Sza.1, "where are you hidden'). To remain silent when things are going against us is for Thérèse to be one with Jesus who was silent before his judges. This is the Holy Spirit's way of conforming us to the Heart of Jesus. Jesus was silent, surrounded by darkness. In the gospel of Luke we read: "This is your hour, this is the reign of darkness" (Lk 22:53). Yet this was the time Jesus shared his purest love. This silence of Jesus is our model for the total surrender of ourselves ('abandon') to God. The world likes those things that glitter. The suffering servant belongs to another order of reality. He does not conform to the pattern of this present world. Jesus has come among us as the one who 'though in the form of God, did not think equality with God a thing to be grasped, but humbled himself, taking the form of a slave' (Phil 2:6-7). We must imitate this 'hiddeness' of Jesus we must allow our lives to be hidden in God: "We must be like Jesus whose face was hidden . . ." In our life with God given over in sweet surrender God allows his love to work. The discovery of who Jesus is, is to meditate on the mystery of his Paschal sacrifice - his journey from Gethsemane to Calvary, ending with the triumph of Easter day. Love conquers the darkness and restores harmony between God and human beings, if we let him in. The love of Jesus is the conqueror because it proceeds from a source that the Heart of Darkness cannot touch. Jesus has given us the Holy Spirit as the fruits of his conquering death, but we are only at the dawn of his complete victory. He calls souls to work with him in the Spirit so that the Heart of Darkness be vanquished and the reign of Love be supreme.

Thérèse gives Céline her experience. Whomever gives his or her life totally manifests the life of Jesus. It is in his self-giving on the Cross that he shows the fullness of his love. The world which has other attractions, this love is 'hidden' because those who follow other ways, such as money, power, glory, sex do not want to see. Those who overcome selfishness and are filled with the

Holy Spirit walk a different way, Thérèse lives in the world of hope that in the end Love will overcome the Darkness and there will be peace in God for all. At the end of 1893 Thérèse has abandoned herself to Jesus - she is in his hands.

The Death of Louis (July 29, 1894)

Thérèse describes how Louis passed away, his long vigil over. She says:

Last year, July 29, God broke the bonds of His incomparable servant and called him to his eternal reward; at the same time He broke those who still held His dear fiancée in the world because she had accomplished her mission. Having been given the office of representing us all with our Father whom we so tenderly loved, she had accomplished this mission just like an angel. And angels don't remain (82v°) on earth once they've fulfilled God's will, for they return immediately to Him, and this is why they're represented with wings. Our angel also spread her white wings; she was ready to fly far away to find Jesus, but He made her fly close by. He was content with simply accepting the great sacrifice which was very painful for little Thérèse. Her Céline had kept a secret hidden from her for two full years. Ah, how Céline herself had suffered because of this! Finally, from heaven my dear King, who never liked stragglers when he was still with us on earth, hastened to arrange Céline's muddled affairs, and she joined us on September 14!

In the earlier version, troubles by other, we read the account of Louis' death in the following words:

During the two preceding Papa's death, Uncle kept him in his own home, taking care of him in his old age. We were able to see him only once during the whole course of his illness because he was so weak. Ah! What a visit that was! You recall it, Mother! When he was leaving and we were saying goodbye, he lifted his eyes to heaven and remained that way a long time and had only one word with which to express his thoughts: "In heaven!" (Histoire d'une Ame).

Céline's muddled mind concerned Fr. Pichon's hope that she go to Canada to help him in his project, but Céline was persuaded by Thérèse's letter and entered Carmel. The above quotation from Histoire d'un Ame shows Pauline's influence.

Chapter Three
<u>Love and Mercy</u>

"My dear friends,
let us love one another
since love is from God.
And everyone who loves is a child of God
and knows God.

Whoever fails to love does not know God
because God is love.
This is the revelation of God's love for us,
that God sent his son into the world
so that we may have life through him.
Love consists in this:
it is not we who loved God
but God loved us first and sent his son
to expiate our sins"   (1 Jn 4: 7-10)

Pope John Paul II made Thérèse a doctor of the church on 19th October, 1997. In the apostolic letter, Divini Amoris Scientia, he says: "During her life Thérèse described, 'new lights, hidden and mysterious meanings' (MsA, 83v°) and received from the divine teacher that 'science of love' which she then expressed with particular originality in her writings (cf MsB, 1r°). This science is the luminous expression of her knowledge of the mystery of the kingdom and her personal experience of grace. It can be considered a special charism of Gospel wisdom which Thérèse, like other saints and teachers of faith, attained in prayer (cf MsC, 36r°)" (Divini Amoris Scientia, no.1). John Paul II here tells us that Thérèse had her own 'particular' insight which helps us appreciate her originality. Later he says: "Even though Thérèse does not have a true and proper doctrinal corpus, nevertheless a particular radiance of doctrine shines forth from her writings, which, as if by a charism of the Holy Spirit, grasps the very heart of the message of Revelation in a fresh and original vision, presenting a teaching of eminent quality" (Divini Amoris Scientia, no.8).

The passage from John tells us God is 'love' and it is from this love we know God. Thérèse never left any written work on this part of the letter of John. Yet all her life and writings were permeated by the Spirit of Love and she led us to appreciate this message 'in a fresh and original vision'. Rudolf Bultmann wrote on the Greek word 'ginosko' (to know) in the Theological Dictionary of the New Testament (TDNT), vol. 7, pp.689-719). He speaks of knowledge (gnosis) in the Gospel and Epistles of John. Apart from its ordinary use the word, gnosis here denotes the relationship to God and to Jesus as a personal fellowship in which each is decisively determined by the other in his own existence. As the relationship between the Father and the Son, which is described elsewhere as 'to be in' (einaen), (Jn 10:38; 14:11; 17:21; cf 1 Jn 2:3 and 5:20) is a mutual knowing (ginoskein), so is the relationship between Jesus and his own (Jn 15:ff; 17:21) 'Eternal life' is to know God and Jesus Christ (Jn 17:3). Thus this knowing is the supreme end time mode of being. This form of knowing is love and God is love (1 Jn 4:8, 16). To be determined by love is thus a criterion of the knowledge of God (1 Jn 4:7f, cf 4:20f), as also of belonging to Jesus (Jn 13:35). Jesus tells us love one another as he has loved us (13:34). Loving determines the relationship between the Father and the Son (13:1, 34; 14:21ff; 15:12, 17). Knowing and loving God achieves expression in concrete facts.

The love of God for the world is actualised in the sending of the Son (Jn 3:16, 1 Jn 4:9ff) and the love of Jesus is his obedience to the Father and in serving his brothers and sisters (1 Jn 2:3-5 cf 3:6). The saying, "Remain in my love" (Jn 15:9) can mean both abiding or remaining (meneir) in being loved and in loving (Jn 17:26; 1 Jn 4:16). The phrase "just as I have loved you! (Jn 13:34; 15:12) means as Bultmann says in his translation "on the basis of the fact that I have loved you." This means that 'knowing' has the sense of recognition of and acceptance of love (i.e. faith, 'pistis' in Greek). This is what brings life to all humankind (see Bultmann, 'ginosko', TDNT 1, p. 711). The Holy Spirit is the bond of love between Father and Son. He was the one promised by Jesus (Jn 14:16-21). Thérèse never wrote as Bultmann did (Indeed she said she would have loved to have studied the scripture in Hebrew and Greek to get back to the original meaning, (D.E 5.8.4, cf Divini Amoris Scientia, no.7, see also "Conseils et souvenirs de Soeur Geneviève, 1989, p.80f). Yet she lived out deeply this message of love and she communicated this message in her own original way.

In Thérèse's time reading of the Bible was not widely encouraged. It was with the publication of Dei Verbum (1965) from the Second Vatican Council that Bible study was given a huge impetus again in the Catholic Church. Having said this I remember when I started reading the Bible as a teenager I was still told this was very 'protestant'. Years later I gave a retreat to a convent of nuns. One sister told me how she 'smuggled' a Bible into the convent when she was younger and she used to read it with the aid of a flash light when lights out was called! This helps us appreciate Thérèse's originality more. For Thérèse, Jesus, who revealed the love of God in person, was the true interpreter of scripture for her. He was the 'Word of God' made flesh (see Jn 1:14), and now by the power of the Holy Spirit he explained the word of God in scripture to Thérèse.

Trust in God

Jesus said, "Do not let your hearts be troubled. You trust in God, trust also in me" (Jn 14:1). In the Last Conversations (DE), Sr. Thérèse of St. Augustine remembers this conversation with Thérèse where Thérèse said "I can assure you that there wasn't a day without suffering, not a single day". Her friend said "But some think you had none". Thérèse answered "Ah! The judgements of creatures! Because they don't see, they don't believe" (Last Conversations, p. 268). During her early years in Carmel, Thérèse felt dryness and loneliness, yet she trusted in God who was quietly performing his work in her suffering. Her trust was in God. The words of Psalm 62 were lived by her:

> "In God alone is my soul at rest;
> my help comes from him.
> He alone is my rock, my stronghold,
> my fortress; I stand firm" (Ps 62:1f)

Thérèse gave herself to God in confidence in the midst of darkness. From 1894 onwards we begin to see the fruits of God's work in Thérèse and from her to us. As we saw, 1894 saw the passing of Louis. Thérèse wrote to Leonie saying: "Papa's death does not give me the impression of a death but of a real life. I am finding him once more after an absence of six years. I feel him around me, looking at me and protecting me. . . (LT 170, Aug 20th). Louis was still inspiring Thérèse. The words of scripture were lived at this time by Thérèse and her sisters and indeed throughout their lives.

> "In all truth I tell you
> you will be weeping and wailing
> while the world will rejoice.
> But your sorrow will turn them to joy"   (Jn 16:20)

Another text from St. Paul shows us how God works quietly, even and especially in our sorrows and for Thérèse in her feeling empty and her 'night of faith'. "We are well aware that God works with those who love him, those who have been called in accordance with his purpose, and turns everything to their good" (Rom 8:28).

1894 also saw the entrance of two important figures to Carmel. One was Sr. Marie of the Trinity on 16th July and the other was Céline (now called Sr. Geneviève of the Holy Face) on 14th September. Céline brought with her a notebook with a list of scriptural references. This was to be a treasure trove for Thérèse. Finally in the winter of 1894 Marie (now Sr. Marie of the Sacred Heart) asked Mother Agnes to tell Thérèse to write her memories of childhood. This manuscript became known as Manuscript A. The "Story of a Soul" is really three manuscripts (A, B and C).

The 'Abandon' of Jesus and Thérèse

Thérèse's letters of 1894 are the ones that allow us a privileged meeting with Thérèse's thoughts. On 21st January 1894 she wrote to Mother Agnes sharing the tension between Jesus' birth and the fate that lay before him. In it Thérèse takes her writing style to a new vertical style of handwriting. This signals that she is changing. In this poem she imagines the dreams of the infant Jesus in the crib. She wrote of this for her sister's feast day.

> However, the night has come. The moon sends out its silvery rays, and the gentle Child falls asleep . . . . His little hand does not let go the flowers that delighted Him during the day, and His Heart continues dreaming about the happiness of His dear spouse.

> Soon, He sees in the distance strange objects bearing no resemblance to the springtime flowers. A cross! . . . A lance! . . . A crown of thorns! And yet the divine Child does not tremble; this is what He chooses to show His spouse how much He loves her! . . .But still it is not enough; His infant face is so beautiful. He sees it disfigured, covered with blood! . . . Unrecognizable! . . . Jesus knows that His spouse will always recognize Him, that she will be at His side when all others abandon Him, so the divine Child smiles at this bloodstained image, He smiles at the chalice filled with the wine giving birth to virgins. He knows that, in His

Eucharist, the ungrateful will desert Him; but Jesus is thinking of His spouse's love, her attention. He sees the flowers of her virtues as they scent the sanctuary, and The Child Jesus continues to sleep on peacefully . . . . He awaits the shadows to lengthen . . . The night of life to give way to the bright day of eternity! . . .   (LT 156).

Jesus has come to reveal the Father's love. In a letter to Céline later in the year (26th April) she asks: "Jesus why did you make yourself so small? For love". Here she shares the words of St. Bernard. Jesus loves by descending, taking the form of a poor little one. He gives away all his love. This helps Thérèse give all to God. She also helps Céline when it was shared with her struggles.

Let the little exile be sad without being sad, for if the tenderness of creatures is not concentrated on her, the tenderness of Jesus is totally CONCENTRATED on her. Now that Céline is without a home, Jesus Himself is well lodged. He is content to see His dear spouse wandering, this pleases Him! Why? . . . I myself know nothing about it . . . . This is Jesus' secret, but I believe He is preparing very beautiful things in His little house . . . He has to work so much that He seems to forget His dear Céline . . . But, no, without being seen by her, he is looking at her through the window. . . . He is pleased to see her in the desert, having no other duty but to love while suffering, without even feeling that she loves! . . . Jesus knows that life is only a dream, so He is taking delight in seeing His spouse weeping on the banks of the river of Babylon! Soon the day will come when Jesus will take His Céline by the hand and will have her enter her little house which will have become an eternal palace . . . . Then He will say: "'Now, my turn.' You have given me on earth the only home that every human heart is unwilling to renounce, that is, yourself, and now I am giving you as a dwelling my eternal substance, that is, "Myself." This is your house for all eternity. During the night of life, you have been homeless and solitary, now you will have a companion, and it is I, Jesus, your Spouse, your Friend, for whom you sacrificed all, who will be this Companion, who must fill you with joy from age to age! . . ." (LT 157)

Thérèse shows Céline that she is favoured to see that the sorrow we have now will be transformed into joy when we see Jesus face to face.

Thérèse writes again on 7th July to Céline. The letter is full of Biblical quotations. We see here her deepening insight into the Person of God. All the mysteries tell us that God is totally other. Yet in reality we do not take this on board. We insist on making God like us. We create Him in our image. He is total love, we are not. Yet we imagine He is like us. Paul Tillich defined faith as the courage to accept acceptance. It requires courage because deep down we do not love perfectly and we fear that God is like us. Yet in God we are totally accepted and loved. He hopes to make us like Him not vice-versa. Thérèse is on a journey to know God. As we accompany her in prayer, many of us find we do not love either ourselves or others as we would like. Thérèse is the one who takes us by the hand to heal us of this fear. Thérèse, at this experienced an inner turmoil 'at least in darkness' (LT 165). Hardly had she set out on her exodus along an unknown path when she is galloping along.' 'I no longer knew who I was' (LT 164). However, a gentle voice is heard, a voice more gentle than the breeze (an image used by Thérèse in her play Joan of Arc) which softly speaks the words, "Return, return". The Holy Spirit groans within her. The hour is approaching when she will make her discovery. But now back to her conversation with Céline.

For Thérèse, Jesus was the Emmanuel (God with us). He is a living God who came to us and entered without any power or protection into the distress of humanity. He is the one who heals us and is with us in our trials. She uses an image from the Canticle of Canticles as an image for the evil, the heart of darkness that dwells in our world.

> I do not know if you are still in the same frame of mind as the other day, but I will tell you just the same about a passage from the Canticle of Canticles which expresses perfectly what a soul is when plunged into aridity and how nothing delights or consoles it. "I went down into the garden of nuts to see the fruits of the valley, to look if the vineyard had flourished, and if the pomegranates had budded . . . I no longer knew where I was . . . My soul was all troubled because of the chariots of Aminadab"   (LT 156)

She goes on to say that this journey for her and Céline is like the soul called to a valley but they find instead of light, darkness.

> This is really the image of our souls. Frequently, we descend into the fertile valleys where our heart loves to nourish itself, the vast

field of the scriptures which has so many times opened before us to pour out its rich treasures in our favour; this vast field seems to us to be a desert, arid and without water . . . . We know no longer where we are; instead of peace and light, we find only turmoil or at least darkness . . . . But, like the spouse, we know the cause of our trial: our soul is troubled because of the chariots of Aminadab . . . . We are still not as yet in our homeland, and trial must purify us as gold in the crucible. At times, we believe ourselves abandoned. Alas! The chariots, the vain noises that disturb us, are they within us or outside us? We do not know . . . But Jesus really knows. He sees our sadness and suddenly His gentle voice makes itself heard, a voice more gentle than the springtime breeze: "Return, return, my Sulamitess; return, return, that we may look at you! . . ." What a call is that of the Spouse! . . . And we were no longer daring even to look at ourselves so much did we consider ourselves without any splendour and adornment; and Jesus calls us, He wants to look at us at His leisure, but He is not alone; with Him, the two other Persons of the Blessed trinity come to take possession of our soul . . . . Jesus had promised it in days gone by when He was about to re-ascend to His Father and our Father. He said with ineffable tenderness: "If anyone loves me, he will keep my word, and my Father will love him, and we will come to him, and we will make in him our abode." To keep the word of Jesus, that is the sole condition of our happiness, the proof of our love for Him. But what, then, is this word? . . . It seems to me that the word of Jesus is Himself . . . He, Jesus, the Word, the Word of God! He tells us further on in the same gospel of St. John, praying to his Father for His disciples, He expresses Himself thus: "Sanctify them by your word, your word is truth." In another place, Jesus teaches us that He is the way, the truth, the life. We know, then, what is the Word that we must keep; like Pilate, we shall not ask Jesus: "What is Truth?" We possess Truth. We are keeping Jesus in our hearts! . . . Often, like the spouse, we can say: "Our Beloved is a bundle of myrrh," that He is a spouse of blood for us. . . . But how sweet it will be to hear one day this very sweet word coming from the mouth of our Jesus: "You are the ones who have always remained with me in all the trials I have had, so I have prepared my kingdom for you, just as my Father has prepared it for me."

Here Thérèse quotes John 14:23 on the indwelling of God in our hearts. This text is more fully described in her poem Vivre d'Amour (PN 15, Feb. 26th, 1895). She also quotes John 17:7, 14:6 and 13: 8. If anyone loves Jesus, according to Thérèse they will keep his word to love one another as he loves them. We can allow and welcome Jesus. He is the one who stands at the door and knocks (Rev. 3:20) and we can let our hearts be a home for him. In one of the pieces Thérèse wrote for recreation, Les Anges à la Crèche de Jésus (The Angels at the Crib of Jesus) RP2, she puts these words into Jesus' mouth "The littlest soul that loves Me - Becomes a Paradise for Me" (Christmas, 1894).

Jesus is with us even in the seemingly darkest moment of our existence. This presence is often 'hidden', to use a word of Thérèse. Yet Thérèse can affirm for us that this presence is real and He is working is us. This shows the confidence and abandonment of faith - we are loved, and we can return home by allowing God to work in us.

Thérèse realises that Jesus, too, came with love but the world he found was alienated from God. Thérèse reflects on his trials and how he asks some special souls to be with him in his lonely agony. Georges Bernanos (1888-1948) brings this out in his characters in such books as "Joy" and "Diary of a Country Priest". Thérèse shares her thoughts with Céline:

The trials of Jesus, what a mystery! He has trials then, He too . . . . Yes, He has them, and often He is alone in treading the wine in the wine press; He looks for consolers and can find none. . . . Many serve Jesus when he is consoling them, but few consent to keep company with Jesus sleeping on the waves or suffering in the garden of agony! . . . Who, then, will be willing to serve Jesus for Himself? . . . Ah! We shall be the ones . . . . Céline and Thérèse will unite always more and more; in them, will be accomplished this prayer of Jesus: "Father, that they may be one as we are one." Yes, Jesus is already preparing His kingdom for us, just as His Father prepared it for Him. He prepares it for us by leaving us in the trial. He wills that our face be seen by creatures, but that it be as though hidden so that no one recognise us but Himself alone! . . . But what joy, too, to think that God, the entire Trinity, is looking at us, that It is within us and is pleased to look at us. But what does It will to see in our heart if not "choirs of music in an army camp"? "How, then, shall we be able to sing the Lord's canticles in a strange land? . . . For a long time, our harps were hung on the willows of the shore." We were not able to use them! . . . Our God, the Guest of our soul, knows it well, so He comes to us with the intention of finding an abode, an EMPTY tent, in the midst of the earth's field of battle. He asks only this, and He Himself is the Divine Musician who takes charge of the concert. . . . Ah! If only we were to hear this ineffable harmony, if one single vibration were to reach our ears! . . .

Thérèse sees herself as someone who welcomes God into their heart so that she can be one with him and allow His love to pour out onto others in whatever way he wishes. The true ones who are children of God are those moved by the Spirit of God. For Thérèse love consists in the permanent attitude of abandonment and the attitude of a trusting child which places itself in the arms of her Father (cf MsC, 25r°). Thérèse loves God by accepting being loved, in accepting acceptance. Thérèse quotes St. Paul in this letter. She says: "We do not know how to ask for anything as we ought, but the Spirit pleads within us with unutterable groanings". This is from Romans 8:26. We love when we allow God in the Spirit to transform us into His love. We have to have the courage to accept being loved and accepted and allow this love to flow to others. Thérèse tells Céline: "We have then, only to surrender our soul, to abandon it to our great God". (LT 154). She is amazed at the self-giving of God that He lives in us. Our God is one who is not afraid to love and live in the hearts of fragile people, ones who are obscure and failing, and they are also created by the hand of God.

Thérèse describes the prayers she read in other books but she says of herself: ". . .I just say simply to God what I wish to say, without composing beautiful sentences and He always understands me. For me, prayer is an aspiration of the heart, it is a simple glance directed to heaven, it is a cry of gratitude and love in the midst of trial as well as joy, it is something great supernatural which expands my soul and unites me to Jesus (MsC, 25r° - 25v°). This powerful meditation of Thérèse leads her to deep understanding of mercy which will come in 1895.

The 'Little' Ones

The prophet Isaiah gives us these words from God: ". . . you are precious in my eyes, and honoured, and I love you" (Is 43:4, NRSV). Isaiah addressed these words originally to a broken people in exile. They are now humble and prepared to receive this word. Over time this saying of Yahweh was extended to all people, culminating in the writings of John where we are told: "God is love" (1 Jn 4:8, 16). Yahweh called his servant to proclaim this message to the people. Later in Deutero-Isaiah we hear the servant speak.

"Coasts and islands, listen to me,
pay attention, distant peoples.
Yahweh called me when I was in the womb,
before my birth
he had pronounced my name.
He made my mouth like a sharp sword,
he hid me in the shadow of his hand.
He made me into a sharpened arrow
and concealed me in his quiver.
He said to me, 'Israel, you are my servant,
through whom I shall manifest my glory.'
But I said, 'My toil has been futile,
I have exhausted myself for nothing,
to no purpose.'
Yet all the while
my cause was with Yahweh
and my reward with my God.
And now Yahweh has spoken,
who formed me in the womb
to be his servant,
to bring Jacob back to him
and to re-unite Israel to him;
- I shall be honoured in Yahweh's eyes,
and my God has been my strength."   (Is 49:1-6)

It is by God's choice that the servant is called. The servant imagines that he is not achieving anything but his cause is with God and he is seen ultimately to truth. God reminds the servant and the people of his care. The prophet tells us of the saying of God for all his people.

"Zion was saying,
'Yahweh has abandoned me,
the Lord has forgotten me.'

Can a woman forget her baby at the breast,
feel no pity for the child she has borne?
Even if these were to forget,
I shall not forget you.
Look, I have engraved you
on the palms of my hands,
your ramparts are ever before me."   (Is 49:6-11)

The important texts from Isaiah for Thérèse were Is 40:11; 66:12-13. I say important because, as we will see, they are the ones she directly quotes. The ones I have used here show us the maternal face of God and His loving kindness. This is the God Thérèse came to know. Her 'little way' made access to the true God accessible for all. The negative image of God was displaced by the gentle-hearted, but tough-minded Thérèse who sought to know the truth of God. Jesus told his followers to be 'wise as serpents and innocent as does' (Mt 10:16). Martin Luther King (1929-1968) in his work "Strength to Love" interprets this saying of Jesus to mean 'the doe stands for the gentle heart, but the serpent the tough mind.' Thérèse had a deep penetrating intelligence which, guided by God's Spirit, leads to understand God in her heart and with her mind. I see this most clearly in something Thérèse said to her sister Marie (Sr. Marie of the Sacred Heart) in the Last Conversations. Marie had told Thérèse that the angels would come resplendent with light and beauty when she died. Thérèse said: "All these images do me no good: I can nourish myself on nothing but the truth" (DE 5.8.4). This was at the time that people like Nietzsche, Freud and many physicists thought the same thing.

The Poor - Little Ones

Thérèse always helps me re-discover what is in scripture. Sacred Scripture is the word of God. In it God communicates with us. It is a drama in which we are involved. When the prophets spoke, it was God who spoke through them. Even though their message was given to a specific people at a specific time their message and challenge are timeless. When God speaking through the prophets challenges the people, He also challenges us. For Thérèse, Jesus was the interpreter of Scripture for her. He was the 'word made flesh' and shared the heart of love of God. In Thérèse's hours before the Blessed Sacrament, her prayerful reading of the word and her abandonment and self-surrender, she allowed Jesus by the power of the Holy Spirit to penetrate to the deep meaning of God's word and she came to know his heart of love.

In the gospel of Matthew we have Jesus instructing his disciples in the Sermon on the Mount. When I read Jesus' instructions I see them alive in Thérèse. In Matthew 5:3-11 we have Jesus' teaching of the Beatitudes. This parallels the teaching of the prophet Isaiah in Is 61. Some of the parallels are more certain than others. Is 61:1-3 reads:

> The spirit of Lord Yahweh
> is on me
> for Yahweh has anointed me.
> He has sent me to bring the news
> to the afflicted,
> to soothe the broken-hearted,
> to proclaim liberty to captives,
> release those in prison,
> to proclaim a year of favour from Yahweh
> and a day of vengeance for our God,
> to comfort all those who mourn
> (to give to Zion's mourners),
> to give them for ashes a garland,
> for mourning-dress, the oil of gladness,
> for despondency, festal attire;
> and they will be called
> 'terebinths of saving justice',
> planted by Yahweh to glorify him.

Now we can look at the parallels. (see Table opposite (Davies and Allison, Matthew 1-7, p. 436f)).

In Isaiah 61, the Spirit of Yahweh has anointed the prophet. He has been sent to bring the good news to the afflicted, to soothe the broken-hearted and to comfort all who mourn (61:1f). This text is fulfilled in a powerful way by Jesus. This is the reason for the blessedness or happiness of the poor, and those who mourn. God's love is present in Jesus to reach out and touch the hearts of the broken. The word for 'blessed' or 'happy' in Greek is 'makarias'. The Greek word means free from daily cares and worries. The Old Testament has its beatitudes or blessings in which the key words are 'ashre' or 'baruk'. The people are blessed because God's salvation and healing is at hand. The first beatitude says: 'Blessed are the poor in spirit' (Mt 5:3). This overturns a popular secular sentiment: 'Blessed are the rich'. The word for poor in Greek

Mt 5	Isa 61
'Blessed are the poor in spirit, for theirs is the kingdom of heaven' (v. 3).	'The Spirit of the Lord is upon me, because the Lord has anointed me, to preach good news to the poor' (v. 1; the connection is all the surer since, in the synoptic tradition, 'to preach good news' or 'good news' is so closely bound to the kingdom of God).
'Blessed are those who mourn for they shall be comforted' (v. 4)	'to comfort all who mourn' (v. 2)
'Blessed are the meek, for they shall inherit the earth' (v. 5)	'to preach good news to the poor' (v.7)
'Blessed are those who hunger and thirst after righteousness, for they shall be satisfied' (v. 6)	'Righteousness' occurs three times in Is. 61, in vv. 3, 8, and 11; and in v. 6, God's people will 'eat the wealth of nations'
'Blessed are the merciful, for they shall receive mercy' (v. 7)	No parallel
'Blessed are the pure in heart, for they shall see God' (v. 8)	'to heal the broken-hearted' (v. 1)
'Blessed are the peacemakers, for they shall be called sons of God' (v. 9)	No parallel
'Blessed are those that have been persecuted for righteousness' sake, for theirs is the kingdom of heaven (v. 10)	'Righteousness' occurs three times in Is. 61, in vv. 3, 8, and 11; and 'kingdom of heaven' can be related to the preaching of 'good news'
'Blessed are you when men revile you and persecute you and utter all kinds of evil against you falsely on my account; rejoice and be glad, for your reward is great in heaven, for so men persecuted the prophets who were before you' (vv. 11-12)	'Let my soul be glad in the Lord' (v. 10; cf v. 11).

'ptochos' means one who is poor, needy, dependent on others, a beggar (see TDNT 6, pp. 885-915). It translates various Hebrew words like 'ani' (poor, afflicted, humble), 'dal' (low, weak) and 'elyon' (needy, poor). Already in the Old Testament, especially in the Psalms the Greek word and its Hebrew equivalents refer to those in special need of God's help (e.g. Ps 12:5; 14:6, 22:34; 37:14; 69:29; 70:5; 86:1; 88:15, Is 61:1) and in time 'poor comes to be a self-designation of the meek, humiliated and oppressed people of God (e.g. Is 10:2; 26:6). In Is 54:11 Jerusalem is the poor one. This is the sense of which 'poor' is used in the beatitudes (c.f. also Mt 11:5; Lk 4:18; 7:22). However this does not mean that the economic idea of 'poor' is excluded. Rather the two go hand in hand. In such texts as Mt 11:5; Lk 4:18; 7:22 we see that Jesus himself and his followers saw their earthly ministry as a fulfilment of Is 61:1-2.

Matthew's addition of the words 'in spirit' does not change anything said above. The addition focuses us on the spiritual meaning as well as the economic (see Jacques Dupont, Les Béatitudes, 3: 385-471). Ultimately, the poor are those who are exiled by the Holy Spirit. Theirs is the kingdom of heaven. Here the world's order is turned upside down: 'those who are at the top here are at the bottom there and those who are at the bottom here are at the top there' (Pesah 50a; c.f. Mt 19:30; 20:16). Even now the kingdom is theirs by the passion of the Holy Spirit.

In chapter 23 Jesus reproaches the Pharisees for their pride and arrogance (Mt 23:1-7). Rather Jesus tells his disciples 'the greatest among you must be your servant. Anyone who humbles himself will be raised up' (Mt 23:11f). This is consistent with the idea of the beatitudes and Jesus' later teaching on the need to become as a little child (see Mt 18:3). Now love and service of our neighbour is placed centre-stage.

Spiritual poverty means being able to say no at living our lives out of selfishness and centring our lives on the love of God and our neighbour. Rene Coste says that another name for spiritual poverty is spiritual infancy of spiritual childhood (Réne Coste, Le Grand Secret des Béatitudes, p. 165). He quotes St. Thérèse who said: "Jesus is pleased to show me the only road which leads to the divine presence and this road is the abandonment of the little child who sleeps without fear in his Father's arms . . ." "Whoever is a little one, let him come to me" (Proverbs 9:4). Said the Holy Spirit through Solomon and the Spirit of the Lord has said again: "Mercy is granted to the little ones" (Wisdom 6:7) (LT 195). Maurice Zundel (1897-1975) gave his insight on poverty when he meditated on the life of St. Francis. He says poverty is another name for generosity. In fact it is another name for God - because God is all loving and gives himself away (see La Pierre Vivante, p. 74 also Morale et Mystique, p. 58). He also hated to hear that God permitted evil because when we look at the Cross we see that Jesus, the Son of God suffered a cruel death so as to give life to us, He was one of the victims of the darkness of the world (see Le problème du mal, cited in Rouiller, 2002). God Himself is the God of the beatitudes. Here God is revealed as Father, Son and Spirit.

Matthew shows us, as do others in the Old and New Testament, that God is our model for living this life of love and self-giving. In July 2002, Pope John Paul II, speaking at the International Day for Youth in Montreal, said that the beatitudes showed the way to follow to create a new society and the way to follow to be happy.

In Carmel Thérèse admired greatly Joan of Arc, 1894 had been the year of Joan of Arc in France, and Thérèse composed a number of plays in her honour. In January 1895 Thérèse was close to joining her heroine in being burnt at the stage. During the production there was a fire on the stage and Thérèse's dress nearly caught fire! It was certainly a lively drama! The other sisters saved her this time. Thérèse was very active in community. She was a joker and mimic during recreation. She could imitate the preachers who came to Carmel. For the sisters she would compose her poems to help them celebrate their feast-days and other occasions. These were the little ways Thérèse built up others. Fr. Marie-Eugene (1894-1967) was a Carmelite priest who was a great devotee of Thérèse. He had read a circular necrology of a Sr. Marie-Philomène de Jesus, who died 5th January, 1925. She was Thérèse's companion in the noviciate (1888-1889). She was prone to depression and life for her was very difficult. One day she was oppressed by depression and nervous exhaustion. Thérèse did not know what to say. It was also time for silence. Thérèse went out of her way to meet Marie-Philomène. She radiated a beautiful smile for her. She later testified that this little act of kindness brought her great ease and helped bring her out of herself. (EC 65.9.8).

As we saw Céline entered the Carmel on 14th September, 1894. Initially she received the name Soeur Marie de la Sainte-Face. Eventually in January 1895 she took the name Soeur Geneviève de Sainte-Thérèse. She had her notebook with scriptural quotations. This was heavenly for Thérèse. She found three texts which helped crystallise her vision. They are: 'Whoever is a little one, let him come to me' (Proverbs 9:4), 'Mercy is granted to the little ones' (Wisdom 6:7) and 'As a mother caresses her child, so will I comfort you. You will be carried on her hip and fondled on her lap' (Is 66:13, 12). Thérèse would use these texts in different ways. We already saw her use two of them in LT 195. These texts were very important for Thérèse as she began to articulate the little way. At the start of her letter to Soeur Marie du Sacre-Couer, we find these three quotations (LT 196). Marie, her older sister and godmother, had asked her to explain the little way. During a retreat Thérèse wrote her explanation for Marie. However Marie asked for a further explanation and this was the occasion for Thérèse's letter in September 1896. The letter and Thérèse's explanation here now become known as Manuscript B (MsB) of "The Story of a Soul". To be a little one is key to understanding Thérèse's message. It was her way of being poor in Spirit. The idea of a mother caressing her child and the little ones being called to God showed Thérèse that the little poor ones were the ones who received from God. Thérèse knew, of course, of Jesus' teaching on becoming a little child (see Mt 18:3).

The discovery of these texts led Thérèse to understand this message. She was the depth of God's love. She could see the God of mercy who could forgive those who seem to us to be the most vile and evil of people. God loves all and hopes to heal the lonely and broken, those whose life seems so far away from him. Thérèse already had some intuition of this in the case of Pranzini.

Thérèse's genius lies in the freshness of her approach to scripture and how she experienced God's love through his word in scripture and in her loving union with the Word-made flesh Jesus. Maurice Bellet wrote this of Thérèse: "Thérèse is among those, who are comparatively few, who truly believes that God loves man" (Thérèse et l'illusion, p. 81). Many people say to me God could not love them. These people do not feel they are worth much. They project onto God the rejections they have experienced from others. Into this darkness Thérèse comes gently and teaches those who feel poor, lonely and broken that they are truly loved by God. All of her life has been a journey to this discovery. The word 'mercy' enters more and more into her writings. She had her 'sickness' of scruples and knew the feeling of being far from God. Now she is prepared to share the fruits of her healing and lead others to know the love of mercy and the healing that is God.

In the same series of letters she would write to Marie later in 1896 she had this to say:

" . . . Ah I really feel that it is not this at all that pleases God in my little soul: what please Him is that He sees me loving my littleness and my poverty, the blind hope that I have in His mercy . . . " (LT 197). Thérèse wrote to Céline (Soeur Geneviève as she is now) "But when I said 'My foot has stumbled, your mercy strengthened me! . . . Ps XCIII (Ps 93:18). Yes it suffices to humble oneself, to bear with ones imperfections. That is real sanctity! (LT 243). Also in MsC, 2v° Thérèse says: "I am to bear myself, such as I am with all my imperfections".

George Bernanos (1888-1947) helped me understand Thérèse by his writings. He has these disturbing words:

There is in man a secret, incomprehensible hatred, not only of his fellowmen, but of himself. We can give this mysterious feeling whatever origin or explanation we want, but we must give it one. As far as we Christians are concerned, we believe that this hatred reflects another hatred, a thousand times more profound and lucid: the hatred of the ineffable spirit who was the most resplendent of all the luminaries of the abyss and who will never forgive us his cataclysmic fall. Outside the hypothesis of an original sin, that is, of an intrinsic contradiction within our nature, the notion of man does become quite clear, only it is no longer the notion of man. When this occurs, man has gone straight through the definition of man, like a handful of sand running between his fingers.

(Diary of a Country Priest, p. 29)

Many people indeed are unhappy with themselves. They find they do not live up to the perfect image they have of themselves. Others when they fail cannot forgive themselves. Thérèse points to the love of God and his mercy, which is an expression of this love. In the light of God's loving mercy people see they are accepted as they are. God meets us in our weakness, brokenness. He knows of what we are made. It is in the light of his love that we can accept ourselves and our weaknesses. Paul had to come to terms with his weakness which he described as a thorn in the flesh. He heard the voice of God say: "My grace is sufficient for thee" (2 Cor 12:9). Cardinal Eugenio Pacelli (later Pius XII) described Thérèse as the greatest healer of the 20th Century in 1939. By leading people to God's mercy Thérèse showed the way for us to come to love ourselves as God loves us. This is a great healing.

In her poem "The Canticle of Céline" (PN 18, April 28, 185) she says the sings the song of someone set free by love:

Oh! How I love the mercy of
The Blessed days of my childhood . . .
To protect the flower of my innocence
The Lord has always surrounded me
With love! . . .

Also, despite my littleness
I was truly filled with tenderness.
And the promise slipped from my heart
To wed the King of the elect
Jesus! . . .   (PN 18:1-2)

These ideas were expressed when people were oppressed with Jansenism. Emphasis was placed on the justice of God and the justice was presented in a very harsh, un-empathetic light. Thérèse was able to cut through all this and see the divine mercy revealed in Jesus-Christ as the final word of God to humanity.

In 1895 Thérèse worked on what would be MsA. She begins her work by saying: "I shall begin to sing what I must sing eternally: 'The Mercies of the Lord' (Ps 88:2)" (MsA, 2r°). Thérèse reflected on the lines from St. Paul in the letter to the Romans: "So it is not matter of what a person wants or what any person does, but only of God having mercy" (Rom 9:16). She says:

It is with great happiness, then, that I come to sing the mercies of the Lord with you, dear Mother. It is for you alone I am writing the story of the little flower gathered by Jesus. I will talk freely and without any worries as to the numerous digressions I will make. A mother's heart understands her child even when it can but stammer, and so I'm sure of being understood by you, who formed my heart, offering it up to Jesus!

It seems to me that if a little flower could speak, it would tell simply what God has done for it without trying to hide its blessings. It would not say, under the pretext of a false humility, it is not beautiful or without perfume, that the sun has taken away its splendour and the storm has broken its stem when it knows that all this is untrue. The flower about to tell her story rejoices at having to publish the totally gratuitous gifts of Jesus. She knows that nothing in herself was capable of attracting the divine glances, and His mercy alone brought about everything that is good in her.

(MsA, 3v°)

These words subvert much of what obscured the true message of God in Jesus. God's mercy is given freely. It is when we admit we are poor, we are sinful and that there is much in us that is wounded that God can enter in. We cannot buy grace. Grace, by its nature is freely given. This is why 'the poor in spirit' are blessed. Thérèse believed that life is to trust in this mercy, that is her treasure. (LT 197).

Our Treasure

Our treasure is to know we are loved. We, many of us, are blocked by many memories, harsh words and bad experiences that block this from our view. Abuse and rejection cause deep wounds in the spirit. Thérèse had her struggles with her childhood illnesses and she lived in a harsh, judgemental world, but she was stubborn in her search and eventually she came to know the tender-loving kindness of God. She is like a pioneer who has gone before us to teach us about the true God.

Each of us has to make our own journey to the discovery of love. My own block was the abuse suffered and the wounds are still real. Meditating on Thérèse and learning from her has, at last, seen the wound beginning to heal. Thérèse had experienced three forms of her own weakness. The first was that of her affections. We saw this better when she was young and extraordinarily timid and sensitive. Then there was her moral weakness. We see this after her 'conversion' of Christmas 1886. She had to struggle with the disease of scruples. Finally, she knew her spiritual weakness. She knew this from the family trial and she experienced it in her last illness. Thérèse was a tough-minded realist. She knew well her own weakness and this revealed to her poverty. She was in need of God to be with her. God was her confidence and she abandoned herself to God. She was one of the 'poor in spirit'. Full with the love of Jesus, she always went to him 'with empty hands'. She trusted in his goodness and love. She expressed her confidence in the following words: "One finds a great peace in being absolutely poor, on not counting on anything but the good God (DE 6.8.4). Her total look of being everything of her helps us understand her great trust in the mercy of God. She knows her own smallness and powerlessness. She says: "The almighty did great things and the greatest was to show his littleness, his powerlessness (MsC, 3v°). Jesus came to us with unconditional love. He was also powerless. He came to us as a child to a poor family and all he had to offer was his love. Once again Thérèse reflects on the kenosis of Jesus (Phil 2:6-11). Yet in allowing God work through her Thérèse became a living icon of the love of God for the world. Later many cures after her death she showed that God still works through her (see Guy Gaucher, Je Voudrais Parcourir la terre).

Thérèse wished to become poor as Jesus himself was poor. She wrote to Céline in April 26th 1894 to console Céline. She had become discouraged with her trials and weaknesses. Thérèse says:

> Do not fear, dear Céline, as long as your lyre does not cease to sing for Jesus, never will it break . . . . No doubt it is fragile, more fragile than crystal. If you were to give it to an inexperienced musician, soon it would break; but Jesus is the one who makes the lyre of your heart sound . . . . He is happy that you are feeling your weakness; He is the one placing in your soul sentiments of mistrust of itself. Dear Céline, thank Jesus. He grants you His choice graces; if always you remain faithful in pleasing Him in little things He will find Himself OBLIGED to help you in GREAT things . . . . The apostles worked all night without our Lord and they caught no fish, but their work was pleasing to Jesus. He willed to prove to them that He alone can give us something; He willed that the apostles humble themselves. "Children," he said to them, "have you nothing to eat?" "Lord," St. Peter answered, "we fished all night and have caught nothing." Perhaps if he had caught some little fish, Jesus would not have performed the miracle, but he had nothing, so Jesus soon filled his net in such a way as to almost break it. This is the character of Jesus: He gives as God, but He wills humility of heart . . .   (LT 161)

When we are weak, we know our need of God. Then we can let him in and by his grace become the people he has called us to be. It is when we love unselfishly that we bring love to God and others. This is the source of Thérèse's teaching - she surrendered herself and her weaknesses to God in love so that He could love in her all that He sees. In MsB, Thérèse says: ". . . I am but a poor little thing who would return to nothingness if your divine grace did not give me life from one moment to the next" and "Jesus, I am too little to perform great actions" (MsB, 5v°). She finishes MsB with the following words:

O Jesus! Why can't I tell all little souls how unspeakable is Your condescension? I feel that if You found a soul weaker and littler than mine, which is impossible, You would be pleased to grant it still greater favours, provided it abandoned itself with total confidence to Your Infinite Mercy. But why do I desire to communicate Your secrets of Love, O Jesus, for it was it not You alone who taught them to me, and can You not reveal them to others? Yes, I know it, and I beg You to do it. I beg You to cast Your Divine Glance upon a great number of little souls. I beg You to choose a legion of little Victims worthy of Your LOVE!

When we know that all we have comes from God by grace - even our very existence - then in truth we can know who we are and come to know God as the totally-other who gives us life. When we come to know our failings and hurts then it is not time to despair. This is where we can allow God in and allow Him to love us.

Thérèse knew her own struggle. She was extraordinarily sensitive and knew her own heart from the struggle she had. Now she knows mercy and confidence. She said as she was coming near her end:

"One could believe that it is because I haven't sinned that I have such great confidence in God. Really tell them, Mother, that if I had committed all possible crimes, I would always have the same confidence; I feel that this whole multitude of offenses would be like a drop of water thrown into a fiery furnace. You will then tell the story about the converted sinner who died of love; souls will understand immediately, for it's such a striking example of what I'm trying to say. However, these things cannot be expressed in words." (DE 11.7.6)

In the piece she wrote for recreation, "The Angels at the Crib of Jesus" (RP 2, 7r). Thérèse has the following reflection and question for Jesus.

"Like Magdalene, after being afforded much
loved much . . . While souls seek for you . . .
deign, O Jesus, just one of your looks full
upon them to make them more brilliant than the
stars of heaven!
'I wish to hear your prayer', answers Jesus
Your soul will obtain pardon
I will fill it with light
those who call upon my name.

In October 1895 Mother Agnes (Pauline) entrusted a spiritual brother, L'Abbé Belliere to Thérèse. He was then a seminarian and he asked for a sister to pray for him. Thérèse was delighted and in her letters to him she showed once more her knowledge of the human heart and how to lead that heart away from all that is not of God to the heart of God which is love. In a letter she wrote to him on 21st June, 1897 she says:

Do not think you frighten me by speaking 'about your beautiful, wasted years.' I myself thank Jesus, who has looked at you with a look of love as, in the past, He looked at the young man in the Gospel. More blessed than he, you have answered faithfully the Master's call, you have left all to follow Him, and this is the most beautiful age of your life, at eighteen. Ah! Brother, like me you can sing the mercies of the Lord, they sparkle in you in all their splendour . . . . You love St. Augustine, Saint Magdalene, these souls to whom 'many sins were forgiven because they loved so much.' I love them too, I love their repentance, and especially . . . Their loving audacity! When I see Magdalene walking up before the many guests, washing with her tears the feet of her adore Master, whom she is touching for the first time, I feel that her heart has understood the abysses of love and mercy of the Heart of Jesus, and, sinner though she is, this Heart of love was not only disposed to pardon her but to lavish on her the blessings of His divine intimacy, to lift her to the highest summits of contemplation.

Ah! Dear little Brother, ever since I have been given the grace to understand also the love of the Heart of Jesus, I admit that it has expelled all fear from my heart. The remembrance of my faults humbles me, draws me never to depend on my strength which is only weakness, but this remembrance speaks to me of mercy and love even more.

When we cast our faults with entire filial confidence into the devouring fire of love, how would these not be consumed beyond return?   (LT 247)

Thérèse knew like St. Paul that is when we are weak then we are strong (cf 2 Cor 12:10), because then we can allow God in. Maurice had experienced his weakness and was discouraged but Thérèse pointed out to him that God's mercy is greater than our weakness. Our strength lies in God not in ourselves.

"Vivre D'Amour" - Living on Love (PN 17)

This poem was written by Thérèse in February, 1895. It arose from her long hours spent in Eucharistic adoration. Thérèse begins by showing us the Word incarnate leads us into the life of the Trinity.

On the evening of Love, speaking without parable,
Jesus said: "If anyone wishes to love me
All his life, let him keep my word.
My Father and I will come to visit him.
And we will make his heart our dwelling.
Coming to him, we shall love him always.
We want him to remain, filled with peace,
          In our Love! . . ."

Living on Love is holding You Yourself.
Uncreated Word, Word of my God,
Ah! Divine Jesus, you know I love you.
The Spirit of Love sets me aflame with his fire.
In loving you I attract the Father.
My weak heart holds him forever.
O Trinity! You are Prisoner
          Of my Love! . . .   (PN 17:1-2)

As she prays before the Blessed Sacrament she considers the love Jesus has for her by remaining hidden in the host. She says:

Living on Love is living on your life,
Glorious King, delight of the elect.
You live for me, hidden in a host.
I want to hide myself for you, O Jesus!
Lovers must have solitude,
A heart-to-heart lasting night and day.
Just one glance of yours makes my beatitude.
      I live on Love! . . .

Later on in the poem she sees how to live on love is to wipe the face of the wounded Jesus. She says:

Living on Love is wiping your Face,
It's obtaining the pardon of sinners.
O God of Love! May they return to your grace,
And may they forever bless your Name . . . .
Even in my heart the blasphemy resounds.
To efface it, I always want to sing:
"I adore and love your Sacred Name.
      I live on Love! . . ."   (PN 17:11)

She described earlier how she must bring God's love to the darkness of hearts that do not know love. She said:

Living on Love is sailing unceasingly,
Sowing peace and joy in every heart.
Beloved Pilot, Charity impels me,
For I see you in my sister souls.
Charity is my only star.
In its brightness I sail straight ahead.
I've my motto written on my sail:
      "Living on Love."   (PN 17:8)

Following her teacher John of the Cross she now begins to speak of the dying of love (see Flammes D'Amour, p. 159f). In the final verse she says:

Dying of Love is what I hope for.
When I shall see my bonds broken,
My God will be my Great Reward.

I don't desire to possess other goods.
I want to be set on fire with his Love.
I want to see Him, to unite myself to Him forever.
That is my heaven ... That is my destiny:
Living on Love!!! ...   (PN 17:15)

This 'dying of love' now enters her vocabulary. She is filled with love and wishes others to experience this love too. She also begins to use terms like 'escalator' or lift - she could not use the harsh road of asceticism, she had to depend on Jesus alone to bring her to the heights of love. She gave herself to the work of the Holy Spirit in love - He is the 'living flame of love'.

Love in the Little Things

Even though Thérèse spoke of great things yet for her the real test was how she loved those around her - especially the ones she found difficult. Fr. Marie-Eugene recounts how Thérèse worked with Sr. Marie de Saint Joseph. She worked in the laundry and had her manic way of doing things (Je veux voir Dieu, p. 855 see also DE 13.7.18). She was always looking for help but most of the nuns tried to avoid her. Thérèse helped her and always approached her with gentleness and a loving smile. This smile soothed the wounded soul of Sr. Marie and Thérèse and herself got on well.

Then there was the case of Sister Teresa of St. Augustine. There was something rigid about her that amazed Thérèse. She is the one Thérèse spoke of in MsC, 13v°-14r°). Sister Teresa never knew how she tried Thérèse's patience because Thérèse always had the warmest, most tender smile for her. Thérèse even dedicated her first poem to her. When she read "The Story of a Soul" when it came out after Thérèse's death she did not realise it was she that Thérèse was talking about when she said she found a certain sister very difficult.

We read in MsC, 14r° where Teresa asks Thérèse: "Would you tell me, Sister Thérèse of The Child Jesus, what attracts you so much towards me; every time you look at me, I see you smile?". Ah! What attracted me was Jesus hidden in the depths of your soul; Jesus who makes sweet what is most bitter. I answered that I was smiling because I hoping to see her ..." there Thérèse adds with a little humour (it is understood that I did not add that this was from a spiritual standpoint). The real test of love is how we live that love from day to day. It

139

is in this context that Pius XI said that Thérèse was fulfilling her vocation 'without leaving the common order of things' (AAS 17 (1925) p. 346). He said this at her canonisation.

In 1896 Mother Marie de Gonzague was returned as prioress. She had a difficult personality and was temperamental. She was a very wounded person. After her election there was tension between her and Agnes (Pauline). She kept the title, novice mistress but effectively Thérèse was left in charge of the novices. Thérèse often had to bear the brunt of Gonzague's moods, yet Thérèse loved her and would listen patiently as she often confided in her. Thérèse knew she was a wounded person. One of Thérèse's novices, Marie of the Trinity would sometimes call Marie de Gonzague the 'wolf'. Thérèse asked her not to call Marie de Gonzague this as it was hurtful. Thérèse also remarked when she was young and visited Carmel how Marie de Gonzague would call her 'Thérèsita' - a pet name. Thérèse remembered the affection Marie de Gonzague shared for them. In 1896 Thérèse had already finished MsA and left a copy in Pauline's choir stall. When Marie de Gonzague took over she asked Thérèse to continue to write her reminiscences and this became what we call manuscript C (MsC). Thérèse wrote MsC in June and July of 1897 near the end of her life.

Chapter Four
One with the Crucified

In the letter to the Collosians we read: "In him, in bodily form, lives divinity in all its fullness and in him you too find your own fulfilment, in the one who is head of every sovereignty and ruling force (Col 2:9f). Our hearts thirst for God and in our communion with Jesus we find God and who we truly are. In our union with Jesus we come 'to share the divine nature' (2 Pt 1:4). Thérèse now begins to speak of the 'merciful love' which by the power of the Holy Spirit fills the heart of Jesus and extends from him to all of us.

Our Way to Love

Every person has to find their own way to know God. Thérèse uses symbolic language to point the way. Thérèse found her little way of confidence and love which helped relieve greatly her fears. Thérèse, when she was younger desired to be a great saint like her heroine Joan of Arc (MsA, 32r°). When she comes to write Manuscript C, she says: "You know, Mother, I have always wanted to be a saint. Alas! I have always noticed that when I compared myself to the saints, there is between them and me the same difference that exists between a mountain whose summit is lost in the clouds and the obscure grain of sand trampled underfoot by passers by" (MsC, 2v°). Yet Thérèse refused to be discouraged. She knew God would not inspire her with impossible desires. John of the Cross was her teacher in this: "The more God wishes to give, the more he makes us desire" (Letter XI). Thérèse knew also from experience that never had God made her desire something without giving it to her. (MsA, 71r°). Thérèsc knew her littleness and her weakness - so she had to depend totally on Jesus. She knew her need of grace:

We are living now in an age of inventions, and we no longer have to take the trouble of climbing stairs, for, in the homes of the rich, an elevator has replaced these very successfully. I wanted to find an elevator which would raise me to Jesus, for I am too small to climb the rough stairway of perfection. I searched, then, in the Scriptures for some sign of this elevator, the object of my desires, and I read these words coming from the mouth of Eternal Wisdom: "Whoever is a LITTLE ONE, let him come to me." And so I succeeded, I felt I had found what I was looking for. But wanting to know, O my God, what You would do to the very little one who answered Your call, I continued my search and this is what I discovered: "As one whom a mother caresses, so will I comfort you; you shall be carried at the breasts, and upon the knees they shall caress you. Ah! Never did words more tender and more melodious come to give joy to my soul. The elevator which must raise me to heaven is Your arms, O Jesus! And for this I had no need to grow up, but rather I had to remain little and become this more and more. (MsC, 3r°)

Here Thérèse quotes Proverbs 9:4 and Isaiah 66:13, 12, the texts that focussed her mind. Thérèse had discovered elevators with Celine on their trip to Slaty. Thérèse had thought up to this she had to be great and big to be a saint. Instead she discovered her littleness and weaknesses. Now she realised that all come from the merciful heart of God. When she was humble of heart then God could truly enter in. God is our health and strength.

In MsB when Thérèse speaks of prayer she uses another image to illustrate this humbleness and the action of God which raises us up. She describes herself as a 'weak, little bird with only a light down as covering. I am not an eagle, but I have only an eagles EYES AND HEART. In spite of my extreme littleness I still dare to gaze upon the Divine Sun, the Sun of love and my heart feels within it all the aspirations of an Eagle' (MsB, 4v°-5r°). The little bird is not able to fly. 'At times the little bird's heart is assailed by the storm and it seems it should believe in the existence of no-other thing except the clouds surrounding it' (MsB, 5r°). Thérèse is here referring to her 'night of faith'. She confesses that the little bird often gets distracted from the Sun. She admits that sometimes the little bird sleeps. This is an allusion to the fact that Thérèse sometimes dozed while she prayed. She compares Jesus to an eagle who comes to rescue Thérèse, the little bird.

O Jesus, You little bird is happy to be weak and little. What would become of it if it were big? Never would it have the boldness to appear in Your presence, to fall asleep in front of You. Yes, this is still one of the weaknesses of the little bird; when it wants to fix its gaze upon the Divine Sun, and when the clouds prevent it from seeing a single ray of that Sun, in spite of itself, its little eyes close, its little head is hidden beneath its wing, and a poor little thing falls asleep, believing all the time that it is fixing its gaze upon its Dear Star. When it awakens, it doesn't feel desolate; its little heart is at peace and it begins once again its work of love. It calls upon the angels and saints who rise like eagles before the consuming Fire, and since this is the object of the little bird's desire the eagles take pity on it, protecting and defending it, and putting to flight at the same time the vultures who want devour it. These vultures are the demons whom the little bird doesn't fear, for it is not destined to be their prey but the prey of the Eagle whom it contemplates in the centre of the Sun of Love.

O Divine Word! You are the Adored Eagle whom I love and who alone attracts me! Coming into this land of exile, You willed to suffer and to die in order to draw souls to the bosom of the Eternal Fire of the Blessed Trinity. Ascending once again to the Inaccessible Light, henceforth Your abode, You remain still in this 'valley of tears,' hidden beneath the appearance of a white host. Eternal Eagle, You desire to nourish me with Your divine substance and yet I am but a poor little thing who would return to nothingness if Your divine glance did not give me life from one moment to the next.   (MsB, 5r°-5v°)

When we know who we are, with all our confusion, doubts and wounds, then this is not a cause for despair. Rather it is our source of hope because then we can let God in. This is where the trust and confidence that Thérèse has spoken about comes into play. God is love and is greater than our conscience (cf 1 Jn 3:20). This is where 'abandon' comes into play. We have to have the courage to let ourselves go into the arms of God's mercy. He is our health and strength. This is what Thérèse discovered and lived in a heroic way for the rest of her life. After her death her prayer continued and there are many people who testify to the healing they have received when they asked Thérèse to intercede for them.

Offering to Merciful Love (Feast of the Trinity, 9th June, 1895)

Our times are different from those of Thérèse. There was a heavy emphasis on justice and the justice of God became a terrifying thing for people. Many nuns of the 19th Century offered themselves to justice. Thérèse broke the mould. In

MsA she said: "To me He has granted his infinite mercy, and thought it I contemplate and adore all the other divine perfections. All of these perfections appear to be resplendent with love, even His justice (and perhaps this so even more than the others) seems to be clothed in love" (MsA, 83v°). The justice of God and the mercy of God seem different in our eyes but not for Thérèse. She will refer to the parable of the Prodigal Son and this helps us understand love and justice.

In Luke 15:11-32, we have the story of a son who asks his father for the inheritance that was to come to him. This was to treat the father, as if he were dead in the world of Jesus. The father gives his son his inheritance and allows him to go away. The son has to live with the results of his own actions. This part refers to 'justice'. Then the son sees his plight and comes home. His father welcomes him. This is 'love and mercy'. Thérèse says: "What a sweet joy to think that God is just, I.e., that He takes into account our weakness, that He is perfectly aware of our fragile nature. What should I fear then? Ah! Must not the infinitely just God who deigns to pardon the faults of the prodigal son with so much kindness". Thérèse says: "He is the Just one. (MsA, 83r°-84v°). Here Thérèse is referring to her self-surrender, her act of oblation or consecration to the divine mercy.

She goes on to speak about souls who offer themselves as victims of God's justice. There were several examples over the years of people who did this. But Thérèse asks: "Does not Your merciful love need them (victims) too. On every side this love is unknown, rejected: those hearts upon whom You lavish it in turn to creatures, seeking happiness from them with their miserable affection: they do this instead of throwing themselves into Your arms and accepting You infinite love" (MsA, 84v°).

Here we see Thérèse's determination - love is not loved (Jacopone di Todi) but she will love love and allow it guide her life. She points the way for others to follow.

The Act of Oblation

On Trinity Sunday during mass Thérèse received the inspiration to offer herself to merciful love. She her offering and now we look at the text and its meaning (PN 6). She says on the 9th June We know more than ever "how Jesus desired to be loved" (MsA, 84r°). Thérèse offered herself in order to love Jesus. Jesus' heart is a heart like ours, a human heart, which itself thirsts for the return of love. "A heart like other hearts, full of warm feeling, full of important hope: full of obstinacy. A heart that pines away when it is not loved" (Von Balthasar, Heart of the World, p. 66). This shows the human heart of Jesus which experiences a deep, interior pain because of his great love for God the Father and his people, and because this is increasingly experienced as rejected.

This is the Jesus she came to know. She was determined to release the floodgates of this love.

> O My God! Most Blessed Trinity, I desire to Love You and make You Loved, to work for the glory of Holy Church by saving souls on earth and liberating those suffering in purgatory. I desire to accomplish Your will perfectly and to reach the degree of glory You have prepared for me in Your Kingdom. I desire, in a word, to be a saint, but I feel my helplessness and I beg You, O my God! To be Yourself my Sanctity!

In this invocation of the Trinity, Thérèse expresses her great love for sanctity and for the salvation of all. She does this when she loves and wished to make loved the Lord. In the next text Thérèse speaks to God the Father, the eternal source of life of the Trinity. She speaks to God of 'his Son':

> Since You loved me so much as to give me Your only Son as my Saviour and my Spouse, the infinite treasures of His merits are mine. I offer them to You with gladness, begging You to look upon me only in the Face of Jesus and in His heart burning with Love.

She calls Jesus God's son and her spouse and saviour. This is the same of St. Paul who said, "the son of God who loved me and gave himself for me" (Gal 2:20). God the Father loved Him and gave Himself to us. All love which Thérèse has received is the gift of the Father who gave His son to us and who loves us always through his son by the power of the Holy Spirit.

In her poem, "Why I Love You, O Mary!" (PN 54:22) Thérèse says:

> "You love us, Mary, as Jesus loves us.
> And for us you accept being separated from Him
> To love is to give everything. It is to give oneself"

God loves us through the 'face of Jesus and in his heart being with love'. Thérèse prays that the living flame of love which is the Holy Spirit would enflame her. The Holy Spirit is also called the river of the waters of life.

Before the Father Thérèse is at once poor and powerless, but at the same time Jesus has made her rich. At the end of Manuscript C she quotes in detail Jn 17:4ff. This is where Jesus prays for those the Father has given Him. Jesus says:

"All I have is yours and all you have is mine, and in this I am glorified"   (Jn 17:10)

Thérèse says: "Your words, O Jesus, are mine, then I can make use of them to draw upon the souls to me, the favours of the Heavenly Father" (MsC, 34v°).

In the next part of the offering Thérèse speaks again of the Trinity. She mentions Jesus' presence in the Eucharist:

I offer You, too, all the merits of the saints (in heaven and on earth), their acts of Love, and those of the holy angels. Finally, I offer You, O Blessed Trinity! The Love and merits of the Blessed Virgin, my dear Mother. It is to her I abandon my offering, begging her to present it to You. Her Divine Son, my Beloved Spouse, told us in the days of His Mortal life: 'Whatsoever you ask the Father in my name he will give it to you!' I am certain, then, that You will grant my desires; I know, O my God! that the more You want to give, the more You make us desire. I feel in my heart immense desires and it is with confidence I ask You to come and take possession of my soul. Ah! I cannot receive Holy Communion as often as I desire, but, Lord, are You not all-powerful? Remain in me as in a tabernacle and never separate Yourself from Your little victim.

Thérèse mentions Mary's part. It was before the statue of Our Lady of the Smile that Thérèse and Celine made their act of oblation together. Mother Agnes said that Thérèse always made an offering to God through the hands of Mary (PO, p. 158). Thérèse initially wrote the words 'infinite desires', but a theologian unfortunately changed this to desires. Thérèse had discovered that Jesus had an infinite thirst for love and she wished to love Him with an infinite love. He sends the Spirit into our hearts. As St. Paul says: ". . . the love of God has been poured into our heart by the Spirit given us" (Rom 5:5). At the start of Manuscript B, Thérèse speaks of her hopes which the infinite and of her desires which are greater than the universe (MsB, 2v°-3r°). The most of her desire is to keep Jesus present to her and in her heart. She refers to his presence in the Eucharist. For Thérèse, Mary is the one who carried Jesus. She says:

"O Immaculate Virgin, I understand how your soul
Is dearer to the Lord than his heavenly dwelling.
I can understand how your soul, Humble and Sweet Valley,
Can contain Jesus, the Ocean of Love! . . ."   (PN 54:3)

She goes on to speak of the littleness, the humility of Mary:

"Oh! I love you, Mary, saying you are the servant
of God the when you charm by your humility.
This hidden virtue makes you all powerful.
It attracts the Holy Trinity into your heart.
Then the Spirit of Love covering you with his shadow,
The Son equal to the father became incarnate in you,
There will be a great many of his sinner brothers,
Since he will be called: Jesus, your first-born! . . ."

(PN 54:4)

Mary's total surrender to God allows God to bring healing and salvation to all. Like, St. Clare, Thérèse could give herself to Mary and bear spiritually in her body he who Mary bore physically *(Third letter to Agnes of Prague)*.

After this allusion to the Eucharist, Thérèse now addresses herself to Jesus. Here she meditates on the Cross, the Passion, and the Resurrection and his Sacred Heart:

I want to console You for the ingratitude of the wicked, and I beg of You to take away my freedom to displease You. If through weakness I sometimes fall, may Your Divine Glance cleanse my soul immediately, consuming all my imperfections like the fire that transforms everything into itself.

I thank You, O my God! For all the graces You have granted me, especially the grace of making me pass through the crucible of suffering. It is with joy I shall contemplate You on the Last Day carrying the sceptre of Your Cross. Since You deigned to give me a share in this very precious Cross, I hope in heaven to resemble You and to see shining in my glorified body the sacred stigmata of Your Passion.

After earth's Exile, I hope to go and enjoy You in the Fatherland, but I do not want to lay up merits for heaven. I want to work for Your Love alone with the one purpose of pleasing You eternally.

In the evening of this life, I shall appear before You with empty hands, for I do not ask You, Lord, to count my works. All our justice is stained in Your eyes. I wish, then, to be clothed in Your own Justice and to receive from Your Love the eternal possession of Yourself. I want no other Throne, no other Crown but You, my Beloved!

Time is nothing in Your eyes, and a single day is like a thousand years. You can, then, in one instant prepare me to appear before You.

Here we learn of Thérèse's great wish 'to love Jesus and to make him loved' (LT 220), by consoling his heart and saving the lost. She wishes to remain radically poor, so she can live by grace and love.

Finally the last part is the offering proper. She wishes to make a gift of herself to the 'fire of love' like a holocaust and to receive in herself the waves of infinite tenderness'. This image refers to the Holy Spirit.

In order to live in one single act of perfect Love, I OFFER MYSELF AS A VICTIM OF HOLOCAUST TO YOUR MERCIFUL LOVE, asking You to consume me incessantly, allowing the waves of infinite tenderness shut up within You to overflow into my soul, and that thus I may become a martyr of Your Love, O my God!

May this martyrdom, after having prepared me to appear before You, finally cause me to die and may my soul take its flight without any delay into the eternal embrace of Your Merciful Love.

I want, O my Beloved, at each beat of my heart to renew this offering to You an infinite number of times, until the shadows having disappeared I may be able to tell You of my Love in an Eternal Face to Face!

The Holy Spirit is in person the love of the Father and the Son. He is the fire of love sent by the Father to the church. Thérèse offers herself to God by the power of the Holy Spirit. In the fire of his love she surrenders herself to the merciful love of God. By the grace of the Holy Spirit she gives herself to Jesus whose heart is being with love. She offers herself to the Father through the sacred-heart. She gives herself to the life-flowing love that is God. She says in Manuscript B: "Ah! If all weak and imperfect souls felt what the least of souls feel, that is, the soul of your little Thérèse, not one would despair of reaching the mount of love. Jesus does not demand great actions from us but simply surrender and gratitude" (MsB, 1v°). Thérèse uses the Biblical idea of holocaust to show she is consumed by the fire of love of the Spirit. In her poem "Living on Love" she shows how love casts out fear and transfers her into a new person:

> "Living on Love is banishing every fear,
> Every memory of past faults,
> I see no imprint of my sins.
> In a moment love has burned everything . . .
> Divine Flame, O very sweet Blaze!
> I make my love in your hearth.
> In your fire I gladly sing
> I live on Love! . . ."   (PN 17:6)

In the total gift of herself Thérèse comes to know 'the love of Christ, which is beyond knowledge' (Eph 3:19).

Two years later when she was ill, Pauline (Mother Agnes) asked Thérèse what happened after she made her act of oblation.

I asked her to explain what happened when she made her Act of Oblation to Merciful Love. First she said:

"Little Mother, I told you this when it took place, but you paid no attention to me."

This was true; I'd given her the impression that I placed no importance on what she was saying.

"Well, I was beginning the Way of the Cross; suddenly, I was seized with such a violent love for God that I can't explain it except by saying it felt as though I were totally plunged into fire. Oh! What fire and what sweetness at one and the same time! I was on fire with love, and I felt that one minute more, one second more, and I wouldn't be able to sustain this ardour without dying. I understood, then, what the saints were saying about these states which they experienced so often. As for me, I experienced it only once and for one single instant, falling back immediately into my habitual state of dryness."

And later on:

"At the age of fourteen, I also experienced transports of love. Ah! How I loved God! But it wasn't at all as it was after my Oblation to Love; it wasn't a real flame that was burning me."
(DE, 7.7.2)

She experienced the wound of love that Teresa of Avila and John of the Cross had spoken of. After this she returned to her usual anxiety. The visits of the Holy Spirit strengthened Thérèse but she didn't linger on them. She had great devotion to the Sacred Heart, the Heart burning with love. She wrote of Jesus' heart in her poem, "To the Sacred Heart of Jesus" (PN 23). She speaks of her need to meet this heart of love. She says:

"I need a heart burning with tenderness,
Who will be my support forever,
Who loves everything in me, even in my weakness . . .
And who never leaves me day or night."
I could find no creature
Who could always love me and never die.
I must have a God who takes on my nature
And becomes my brother and is able to suffer! (PN 23:4)

The heart is a Biblical symbol for the inner person. Jesus is all love and Thérèse here describes how she longs to experience that heart. Then she realises her prayer is heard:

You heard me, only Friend whom I love.
To ravish my heart, you became man.
You shed your blood, what a supreme mystery! . . .
And you still live for me on the Altar.
If I cannot see the brilliance of your Face
Or hear your sweet voice,
O my God, I can live by your grace,
I can rest on your Sacred Heart!

O Heart of Jesus, treasure of tenderness,
You Yourself are my happiness, my only hope.
You who knew how to charm my tender youth,
Stay near me till the last night.
Lord, to you alone I've given my life,
And all my desires are well-known to you.
It's in your ever-infinite goodness
That I want to lose myself, O Heart of Jesus!   (PN 23:4-5)

Here she sees how Jesus gives his heart away - he gives us love. There we can rest and find peace. This is the source of our confidence. For Christmas 1895, Thérèse composed a little play, "The Divine Little Beggar" (RP 4). In it the infant Jesus comes to pray for the hearts of the sisters. In this helpless baby God, who has emptied himself (kenosis) begs for human love. Heart speaks to heart in the exchange of love.

In September 1896, Marie (Sr. Marie of the Sacred Heart), Thérèse's oldest sister and godmother asked for her to explain the 'little way' to her. This would become known as part of Manuscript B. Marie did not understand Thérèse so Thérèse composed a body of letter for Marie - LT 196 which forms the first part of Manuscript B. In LT 197, Thérèse would say to Marie:

Oh, dear Sister, I beg you, understand your little girl, understand that to love Jesus, to be His victim of love, the weaker one is, without desires or virtues, the more suited one is for the workings of this consuming and transforming Love. . . . The desire alone to be a victim suffices, but we must consent to remain always poor and without strength, and this is the difficulty, for: "The truly poor in spirit, where do we find him? You must look for him from afar," said the psalmist . . . . He does not say that you must look for him among great souls, but "from afar," that is to say in lowliness, in nothingness . . . . Ah! Let us remain then very far from all that sparkles, let us love our littleness, let us love to feel nothing, then we shall we poor in spirit, and Jesus will come to look for us, and however far we may be, He will transform us in flames of love . . . . Oh! How I would like to be able to make you understand what I feel! . . It is confidence and nothing but confidence that must lead us to Love . . . Does not fear lead to Justice? . . . Since we see the way, let us run together. Yes, I feel it, Jesus wills to give us the same graces, He wills to give us His heaven gratuitously.

Oh! Dear little sister, if you do not understand me, it is because you are too great a soul . . . Or rather it is because I am explaining myself poorly, for I am sure that God would not give you the desire to be POSSESSED by Him, by His Merciful Love if He were not reserving this favour for you . . Or rather He has already given it to you, since you have given yourself to Him, since you desire to be consumed by Him, and since God never gives desires that He cannot realize. . . . (LT 197)

Here Thérèse emphasises her littleness - her nothingness, but she accepts this because the Holy Spirit will transform her in 'flames of love'. Being humble allows her in. It is confidence that leads us to love. This is the heart of the little way. Marie would become the third sister to offer herself to divine love in the summer of 1896. At first she was nervous because she was afraid of suffering. But Thérèse said to her that the offering was in order to love God better for those who do not want to love Him. This won Marie over and she made her Act of Oblation (Notebook of Sister Marie of the Incarnation, June 6th 1934, p. 137).

The Night of Thérèse's Life

Thérèse also saw the mercy of God in the way he kept her away from obstacles that would cause her to fall (MsC, 36v°). It reminds me of a prayer I once heard and often say, "O, Lord save me from myself!" Thérèse knew that God knew us better than we know ourselves and he takes note of our weaknesses, because he made us (MsA, 83v°).

Holy Week 1865 was a major turning point in Thérèse's life. The time leading up to Holy Week had been a relatively happy time for Thérèse. On Holy

Thursday of that year (29th March) Thérèse coughed up blood. She realised that she was ill (MsC, 4v°-5r°). Her illness would get progressively worse over the course of the next eighteen months. The treatment would be old-fashioned and cruel. Thérèse would suffer physically.

However, a still greater cross awaited her on Easter Sunday. All the joy she had known suddenly disappeared without any warning. She felt she was confronted by a wall which reached right up to heaven. She had been joyful at the thought of dying of love. Now horrible voices suggested to her that all her great desire, the little way, her offering, her whole spiritual life, had been illusions. She knew she was going to die young and the voices told her it was all for nothing. She describes the feelings as follows:

At this time I was enjoying such a living faith, such a clear faith, that the thought of heaven made up all my happiness, and I was unable to believe there were really impious people who had no faith. I believed they were actually speaking against their own inner convictions when they denied the existence of heaven, that beautiful heaven where God Himself wanted to be their Eternal Reward. During those very joyful days of the Easter season, Jesus made me feel that there were really souls who have no faith, and who, through the abuse of grace, lost this precious treasure, the source of the only real and pure joys. He permitted my soul to be invaded by the thickest darkness, and that the thought of heaven, up until then so sweet to me, be no longer anything but the cause of struggle and torment. This trial was to last not a few days or a few weeks, it was not to be extinguished until the hour set by God Himself and this hour has not yet come. I would like to be able to express what I feel, but alas! I believe this is impossible. One would have to travel through this dark tunnel to understand this darkness. I will try to explain it by a comparison.

I imagine I was born in a country that is covered in thick fog. I never had the experience of contemplating the joyful appearance of nature flooded and transformed by the brilliance of the sun. It is true that from childhood I heard people speak of these marvels, and I know the country I am living in is not really my true fatherland, and there is another I must long for without ceasing. This is not simply a story invented by someone living in the sad country where I am, but it is a reality, for the King of the Fatherland of the bright sun actually came and lived for thirty-three years in the land of darkness. Alas! The darkness did not understand that this Divine King was the Light of the world.

(MsC, 5r°-6v°)

The world has become dark for Thérèse. It is as if she were in a country 'covered in thick fog'. This was the world Jesus came to but the darkness and the fog blinded people to Him. Thérèse is now united with Jesus in his lonely agony in the world of darkness. I have used the image of the Heart of Darkness to express this 'fog', this lack of light. Jesus came to bring light into darkness. Thérèse was now being called to share in a mystical way in his lonely hours when the darkness seemed to overcome him.

Thérèse goes on to describe her situation. She says: "Your child (Thérèse) however, O Lord, has understood your divine light and she begs pardon for her. She is resigned to eat the bread of sorrow as long as You desire it: she does not wish to rise from the table filled with bitterness at which poor sinners are eating with until the day set by You" (MsC, 6v°). Thérèse now finds herself spiritually in union with those who seem far from God - she is one with the atheists, the lonely, the depressed, those who feel nobody wants them or cares. She is now one of them. She literally feels their pain. It is now her pain. Her ill body and trial of faith become a living prayer of the lonely and comforts those who feel there is no comfort. This is Thérèse's heroic living of the little way which she goes through for the last eighteen months of her life.

Even when she abandons herself to this prayer she still suffers for the darkness of this world. This was what was known as the Diana Vaughan affair. In 1895 a work was published entitled "The Memoirs of an Independent, Fully Initiated ex-Palatine." This was about the conversion of 'Diana Vaughan' from freemasonry and satanic sects. She also published "The Eucharistic Novena of Reparation" in 1895. Thérèse was moved by the spiritual writings of this young woman who loved Joan of Arc so much. Thérèse sent her a picture of herself acting the part of Joan of Arc. Then in April 1897 Diana Vaughan called a press conference to show herself to the world. Nobody allegedly knew much about the mysterious 'Diana Vaughan'. The whole affair proved to be an elaborate hoax played by a man called Leo Taxil. At the press conference the picture of Thérèse was displayed. A humiliating body-blow for one who was praying and suffering for people such as Taxil.

However, Thérèse had written a little play for the nuns in which she had warned them about too much curiosity. The play was called "Dialogue of the Carmelites" (RP 7). In it Thérèse says:

We now know the way to conquer the demon, and so, henceforth let us have but one desire: to practise humility. It is our weapon, our shield. With this all-powerful strength we, like new Joans of Arc will know how to drive the stranger out of the kingdom, that is, to prevent proud Satan from entering into our monasteries.

The final verse directs the community towards the little way:

O fervent Carmelites your will
is to win hearts for your spouse Jesus.
So for him you must stay little,
humility all hell confuses.

Thérèse even composed "The Triumph of Humility" (RP 7) which was based on the memoirs of Diana Vaughan (June 21st, 1896). The Taxil affair showed her how evil and manipulative the heart of darkness can be. Incidentally the name Leo Taxil was not the real name of the impostor. He was a certain Marie-Joseph Jognad-Pages (1854-1907) from Marseilles. He was deeply anti-Catholic.

Thérèse goes on to describe the loneliness of the state she was in, in MsC, 6v°. She says:

I was saying that the certainty of going away one day far from the sad and dark country had been given me from the day of my childhood. I did not believe this only because I heard it from persons much more knowledgeable than I, but I felt in the bottom of my heart real longings for this most beautiful country. Just as the genius of Christopher Columbus gave him a presentiment of a new world when nobody had even thought of such a thing; so also I felt that another land would one day serve me as a permanent dwelling place. Then suddenly the fog that surrounds me becomes more dense; it penetrates my soul and envelops it in such a way that it is Impossible to discover within it the sweet image of my Fatherland; everything has disappeared! When I want to rest my heart fatigued by the darkness that surrounds it by the memory of the luminous country after which I aspire, my torment redoubles; it seems to me that the darkness, borrowing the voices of sinners, says mockingly to me: "You are dreaming about the light, about a fatherland embalmed in the sweetest perfumes; you are dreaming about the eternal possession of the Creator of all these marvels; you believe that one day you will walk out of this fog that surrounds you! Advance, advance; rejoice in death which will give you not what you hope for but a night still more profound, the night of nothingness."

Dear Mother, the image I wanted to give you of the darkness that obscures my soul is as imperfect as a sketch is to the model; however, I don't want to write any longer about it; I fear I might blaspheme; I fear even that I have already said too much. (MsC, 6v°-7r°)

The Mother she addresses in MsC is Marie de Gonzague for whom she wrote Manuscript C. Pauline suggested to Marie de Gonzague that Thérèse continue her writing that she had begun for her. This was in 1897. Thérèse began to write but could only complete two chapters before she became too weak. Here she describes her fatigue caused by nervous exhaustion. There is no relief for her because the voices try to convince her all in useless - give up. She has a true share in Jesus' passion. Her fear of there being no heaven was somewhat relieved by a dream she had. In the dream she saw Anne de Lobera (1543-1621). She was a Carmelite sister and friend of Teresa of Avila. John of the Cross wrote the Spiritual Canticle for her and she brought the reformed Carmel into France.

At the first glimmerings of dawn I was (in a dream) in a kind of gallery and there were several other persons, but they were at a distance. Our Mother was alone near me. Suddenly, without seeing how they had entered, I saw three Carmelites dressed in their mantles and long veils. It appeared to me they were coming for our Mother, but what I did not understand clearly was that they came from heaven. In the depths of my heart I cried out: "Oh! How happy I would be if I could see the face of one of these Carmelites!" Then, as though my prayer were heard by her, the tallest of the saints advanced toward me; immediately I fell to my knees. Oh! What happiness! The Carmelite raised her veil or rather she raised it and covered me with it. Without the least hesitation, I recognized Venerable Anne of Jesus, Foundress of Carmel in France. Her face was beautiful but with an immaterial beauty. No ray escaped from it and still, in spite of the veil which covered us both, I saw this heavenly face suffused with an unspeakably gentle light, a light it didn't receive from without but was produced from within.

I cannot express the joy of my soul since these things are experienced but cannot be put into words. Several months have passed since this sweet dream, and yet the memory it has left in my soul has lost nothing of its freshness and heavenly charms. I still see Venerable Mother's glance and smile which was FILLED with LOVE. I believe I can still feel the caresses she gave me at this time.

Seeing myself so tenderly loved, I dared to pronounce these words: "O Mother! I beg you, tell me whether God will leave me for a long time on earth. Will He come soon to get me?" Smiling tenderly, the saint whispered: "Yes, soon, soon, I promise you." I added: "Mother, tell me further if God is not asking something more of me than my poor little actions and desires. Is He content with me?" The saint's face took on an expression incomparably more tender than the first time she spoke to me. Her look and her caresses were the sweetest answers. However, she said to me: "God asks no other thing from you. He is content, very content!" After again embracing me with more love than the tenderest of mothers has ever given a child I saw her leave. My heart was filled with joy, and then I remembered my Sisters, and I wanted to ask her some favours for them, but alas, I awoke!

O Jesus, the storm was no longer raging, heaven was calm and serene. I believed, I felt that there was a heaven and that this heaven is peopled with souls who actually love me, who consider me their child. (MsB, 2r°-2v°)

Over the eighteen months in which she lived in this darkness she would come close to a nervous breakdown and thoughts of suicide would plague her as she became progressively worse. Pauline recalls the following:

During this phase of her sickness, how many times must her patience have caused God to smile! What sufferings she had to endure! She sighed many times like a poor little lamb about to be immolated. She told me:

"Watch carefully, Mother, when you have patients a prey to violent pains; don't leave near them any medications that are poisonous. I assure you, it needs only a second when one suffers intensely to lose one's reason. Then one would easily poison oneself."

(Last Conversations, p. 258, see also p. 196 and p. 295)

Thérèse lives the pain of the absence of God and experiences this in all its grim reality. Her response is sacrificial love. She affirms God's goodness in the face of evil. She is one with God in bringing light to the deepest darkness - the world of rejection and despair, the world of profound loneliness. Thérèse is prepared to stay here so that those who are broken will receive light and healing. Anybody who knows the pain of darkness, deep depression knows how hard this cross can be. She is in living contact with those who choose to walk ways other than those of light - Taxil's deceit would teach her the reality of this position. She did not really realise that there were souls who did not believe in God - now she did. She knew how they felt. She confided to Mother Agnes: "The worst kind of materialistic arguments came into my mind. Later, science, by making ever-increasing new progress, will explain everything naturally" (see Guy Gaucher, The Story of a Life, p. 162). She was against everybody. She loved them all. She prayed with her body and soul for them. She suffered a sacrifice of love for all (including Taxil!). She surrendered herself like "a soul who searches for God in the night of faith" (PN 54:15) - the true state of 'abandon'. She felt that she would continue her mission for prayer for the broken after death. "I will spend my heaven in doing good for the world" (DE 17:1). Her prayers would be like a shower of roses (DE 9.6.3). Thérèse would bring the novices into the garden to throw petals near the cross - as a symbol of their prayers and offerings. Thérèse knew that in the depths of each person God could dwell - if they let him in. It is by God's grace that Thérèse came to love all people and see His image in them. She lived her night of faith in submission and abandonment to the will of God.

Bernard Sesboüé meditated on the meaning of the cross of Jesus. The passion of Jesus is salvific because in the face of death and hate Jesus brings his love and acceptance. In the end love is stronger than death (see Song of Songs 8:6). To the question: why did the cross have to be so violent? Why did Jesus choose such a way, Sesboüé reminds us that sinful people (pagans and Jews alike) refused the announcement of the Kingdom of God, this caused them to put to death the just one and because they considered the presence of the just one intolerable. (B. Sesboüé, Jesus-Christ, l'unique mediateur, Vol. 1, pp. 62-63)

Thérèse Shares with Jesus in His Passion

Von Balthasar said the following about the humility of the Word, speaking in human suffering, is a direct revelation of the self-giving, unconditional love of God:

> The mistake of the great Alexandrians and their followers was . . . (that they) regarded sense as a prison and a disguise, rather than a means of revealing the spiritual . . . . Their philosophy could not rightly express the Biblical dialectic, for God's "self-emptying," his "becoming poor," is a direct image of his fullness and richness and the prodigality of his love; the spiritual is made known to us through its covering, and is brought close to us through its sensible expression. (Mysterium Paschale, p. 213)

Here we see that for Von Balthasar the revelation of the poverty of Christ is the revelation of the divine abandon. He is poor and powerless because he gives all away in love. This too was the insight of Thérèse. She was united with Jesus in his poverty.

> For in Christ's passion the human senses and spirit were engulfed in the night which extinguished all awareness of the divine, the night in which he was abandoned by the Father, when the human faculties were lost in the void and, deprived of their natural food, succumbed. This did not occur in the realm of philosophy but in the freedom of love taking on itself the consequences of sin. The truth of the negative theology can be seen in the cross which carried it to its furthest limit . . . In that darkness (of hell) he (Christ) liberated the senses and the faculties subject to sin and enabled them to apprehend God in a manner befitting their redeemed state. (Mysterium Paschale, p. 25)

By entering the darkness Jesus brings his light to her. By the power and gift of the Holy Spirit Jesus continues this work in the church. He calls certain souls like Thérèse to join him in his night of faith. Von Balthasar says:

> For if the Son ceases to be a subject of contemplation, it is only to incorporate the contemplative more fully in Christ's own inward state and allow him an active participation in Christ's death and resurrection. Indeed, the mystical night of the senses and the spirit, however solitary the person experiencing them, is always something that bears on the Church, something deeply embedded in the order of the Incarnation. Theology can demonstrate the fact, whereas the mystics, describing their experience of the night, necessarily dwell on the feeling of being alone; that is why they do not always avoid the temptation of using the categories of Platonism to describe their experiences. (Prayer, p. 216)

Complete abandonment to God led Thérèse to an extremity in which God's presence is experienced as a terrible void, an absence in which the soul feels forsaken by God and knows itself as an utter hollowness and extreme thirst that which God alone can assuage. The more Thérèse enters this 'night' the more she enters into the common plight of God's people. In the Ascent to Mount Carmel, John of the Cross says: "Union with God does not consist in recreations, experiences or spiritual feelings, but in the one and only living, sensory and spiritual, exterior and interior, death of the Cross."
(Ascent ii, 7: 8-11).

Von Balthasar describes Thérèse's trial of faith, in the following way:

> Every means of measurement is abandoned and the measure rests with God alone. Nor is this just an episode, a dark but temporary night of the senses or the spirit; it is lasting, unto the end. . . . (Thérèse) goes on striding endlessly in the darkness, below the earth, without bearings. Instead of the satisfaction of climbing higher, she puts one foot in front of the other along a road whose direction God alone knows.
> (Von Balthasar, Thérèse, p. 203)

Thérèse trusts and hopes against hope. She allows God to work through this suffering little servant Thérèse. As St. Paul says: ". . . the Spirit too comes to help us in our weakness for, when we do not know how to pray properly, then the Spirit personally makes our petition for us in groans that cannot be put into words" (Rom 8:26) and later he says, "We are well aware that God works with those who love him, those who have been called in accordance with his purpose and turns everything to their good" (Rom 8:28). Thérèse herself says: "A scholar has said: Give me a lever and a fulcrum and I will lift the world." What Archimedes was not able to obtain for his request was not directed by God and was only made from a material viewpoint, the saint's love obtained in all its fullness. The almighty has given them a fulcrum: HIMSELF ALONE; as lever PRAYER which burns with a fire of love (MsC, 35r°-36v°). The thinking that has to be moved is the mound of doubt, fear and loneliness, the feeling of not being wanted. By Jesus' death and resurrection a new world is heralded in. We are caught in the 'already but not-yet'. We are only at the dawn of the new world where God makes all things new (Rev 21:5).

By her prayer Thérèse works with Jesus in creating the new world where all tears are wiped dry and there is no more darkness (Rev 21:1-4). The heart of darkness will be overcome by love, but we are only yet at the dawn of that age.

Her True Vocation

In September of 1896, as we saw, Thérèse wrote Manuscript B explaining the little way. In it is a passage we have come across often. Thérèse always felt a call to love As a child Thérèse often thought about God (CSG p. 83). For Thérèse God's love was revealed in Jesus and therefore Jesus is all for Thérèse. In union with Him she enters the life of the Trinity and loves with the heart of Jesus. She knew that after death she would see God, but she felt she would only see what she possessed already (NV, p. 6).

Thérèse knew from her experiences at how, during her first communion that she was deeply loved by God. She would say: "I do not see the Sacred Heart as do other people. I think the heart of my spouse is mine only, as is mine for Him. I speak to him in this delightful heart to heart, all the time waiting for the day when contemplate his face to face" (LT 102). Thérèse here says that God's love is so vast, that when we come to know it is as if we were the only people in the world.

The love between Jesus and Thérèse was very tender, loving and inclusive. Thérèse would say:

You know, O my God, I have never desired anything but to love You, and I am ambitious for no other glory. Your Love has gone before me, and it has grown with me, and now it is an abyss whose depths I cannot fathom. Love attracts love, and, my Jesus, my love leaps towards Yours; it would like to fill the abyss which attracts it, but alas! It is not even like a drop of dew lost in the ocean! For me to love You as You love me, I would have to borrow Your own Love, and then only would I be at rest. O my Jesus, it is perhaps an illusion but it seems to me that You cannot fill a soul with more love than the love with which You have filled mine; it is for this reason that I dare to ask You "to love those whom you have given me with the love with which you loved me." One day, in heaven if I discover You love them more than me, I shall rejoice at this, recognizing that these souls merit Your Love much more than I do; but here on earth, I cannot conceive a greater immensity of love than the one which is has pleased You to give me freely, without any merit of my part.

(MsC, 35v°-35r°)

In the light of this loving Thérèse described her vocation. We read:

O my Jesus! What is your answer to all my follies? Is there a soul more little, more powerless than mine? Nevertheless even because of my weakness, it has pleased You, O Lord, to grant my little childish desires and You desire, today, to grant other desires that are greater than the universe.

During my meditation, my desires caused me a veritable martyrdom, and I opened the Epistles of St. Paul to find some kind of answer. Chapters 12 and 13 of the First Epistle to the Corinthians fell under my eyes. I read there, in the first of these chapters, that all cannot be apostles, prophets, doctors, etc., that the Church is composed of different members, and that the eye cannot be the hand at one and the same time. The answer was clear, but it did not fulfil my desires and gave me no peace. But just as Mary Magdalene found what she was seeking by always stooping down and looking into the empty tomb, so I, abasing myself to the very depths of my nothingness, raised myself so high that I was able to attain my end. Without becoming discouraged, I continued my reading, and this sentence consoled me: "Yet strive after THE BETTER GIFTS, and I point out to you a yet more excellent way. And the Apostle explains how all the most PERFECT gifts are nothing without LOVE. That Charity is the EXCELLENT WAY that leads most surely to God.

I finally had rest. Considering the mystical body of the Church, I had not recognized myself in any of the members described by St. Paul, or rather I desired to see myself in them all. Charity gave me the key to my vocation. I understood that if the Church had a body composed of different members, the most necessary and most noble of all could not be lacking to it, and so I understood that the Church had a Heart and that this Heart was BURNING WITH LOVE. I understood it was Love alone that made the Church's members act, that if Love ever became extinct, apostles would not preach the Gospel and martyrs would not shed their blood. I understood that LOVE COMPRISED ALL VOCATIONS, THAT LOVE WAS EVERYTHING, THAT IT EMBRACED ALL TIMES AND PLACES . . . . IN A WORD, THAT IT WAS ETERNAL!

Then, in the excess of my delirious joy, I cried out: O Jesus, my Love . . . . My vocation, at last I have found it . . . . MY VOCATION IS LOVE!

Yes, I have found my place in the Church and it is You, O my God, who have given me this place; in the heart of the Church, my Mother, I shall be Love. Thus I shall be everything, and thus my dream will be realized   .(MsB, 3r°-3v°)

Here Thérèse quotes 1 Cor 12:29, 21, 31 and 13:1. In this part of 1 Corinthians St. Paul speaks of love. There are many ways of reading St. Paul. In chapter 13 he says: "love is always patient and kind; love is never jealous; love is not boastful or conceited, it is never rude and never seeks its own advantage, it does not take offence or store up grievances. Love does not rejoice at wrongdoing, but finds its joy in the truth. It is always ready to make allowances, to trust, to hope and to endure whatever comes. Love never comes to an end" (1 Cor 13:4-8). This is a description of Jesus - the only one to he as Paul describes love. Thérèse saw this too.

Thérèse describes how by looking at Jesus she discovered the true meaning of love.

How did Jesus love His disciples and why did He love them? Ah! It was not their natural qualities that could have attracted Him, since there was between Him and them an infinite distance. He was knowledge, Eternal Wisdom, while they were poor ignorant fisherman filled with earthly thoughts. And still Jesus called them his friends, His brothers. He desires to see them reign with Him in the kingdom of His Father, and to open that kingdom to them He wills to die on the cross, for He said: "Greater love than this no man has than that he lay down his life for his friends."

Dear Mother, when meditating upon these words of Jesus, I understood how imperfect was my love for my Sisters. I saw I didn't love them as God loves them. Ah! I understand now that charity consists in bearing with the faults of others, in not being surprised at their weakness, in being edified by the smallest acts of virtue we see them practice. But I understood above all that charity must not remain hidden in the bottom of the heart, Jesus has said: "No one lights a lamp and puts it under a bushel basket, but upon the lamp stand, so as to give light to ALL in the house." It seems to me that this lamp represents charity which must enlighten and rejoice not only those who are dearest to us but "ALL who are in the house" without distinction.

When the Lord commanded His people to love their neighbour as themselves, He had not as yet come upon the earth. Knowing the extent to which each one loved himself, He was not able to ask of His creatures a greater love than this for one's neighbour. But when Jesus gave His Apostles a new commandment, HIS OWN COMMANDMENT, as He calls it later on, it is no longer a question of loving one's neighbour as oneself but of loving him as He, Jesus, has loved him, and will love him to the consummation of the ages.

Ah! Lord, I know you don't command the impossible. You know better than I do my weakness and imperfection; You know very well that never would I be able to love my Sisters as You love them, unless You, O my Jesus, loved them in me. It is because You wanted to give me this grace that You made Your new commandment. Oh! How I love this new commandment since it gives me the assurance that Your Will is to love in me all those You command me to love!   (MsC, 12r°-12v°)

Here Thérèse quotes John chapter 15, Matthew 5:15 and Leviticus 19:18. Thérèse admits her weakness. She cannot love as Jesus loves. But, in the spirit of abandonment and the little way, she admits her weakness and allows him to draw her up 'on eagle's wings'. Here by the power of the Holy Spirit her heart is transformed.

In her act of surrender to Jesus she lets Him love those around her with his heart - she allows his love to overcome her and flow to others. She was a religious genius who lived an ordinary life.

The Christ-like State of Love

According to Von Balthasar we become truly human when we are drawn out of ourselves by the Word, and answer his call. The model for this becoming fully human in Jesus: "It is precisely in embracing the Father's will that Jesus discovers his own, most profound identity as the eternal Son" (Theo-Drama, III, p. 199f). Jesus loves the Father with his whole heart. The historical dramatic existence of Jesus means the incorporation is a moment-by-moment victory of Jesus' will to love. The more the Son unites himself with the ground for which his person and mission simultaneously spring, the better he understands his mission and himself" (Theo-Drama III, p. 168). By his utter self-abandonment to the Father, his own human capabilities are released into the divine freedom and in this state he is able "by the force of this healing over in resurrection life (sacrament, word and the sending of the Holy Spirit) to become what he should be God and humankind. The resurrected Jesus, by giving himself in love by the power of the Holy Spirit, brings those he calls out of themselves. He draws them to a love and into being-as-communion with Him. (M. A. McIntosh, Christology From Within, p. 128f). Those he called, like Thérèse, are called into the realm of the Spirit. The resurrected state is where Jesus allows his love flow on all humanity. In being-as-communion, being one with His love, Thérèse co-operates in His mission to pour out love on all humankind. Thérèse had a tender-loving relationship with Jesus and she fulfils her life by taking up her particular share in Jesus' mission. In her trial of faith she faced the trial squarely and lived the last eighteen months by faith in love. She never ceased to love even in the deepest darkness. She left the results of this deep prayer to God.

Jean François Six speaks about Thérèse's 'Consecration to The Holy Face' (Lumière de la Nuit, p. 70, ff). This Consecration (pri 12) took place at Easter, 1896 and is an extension of her act of self-oblation. She quotes St. John of The Cross who says "The smallest act of pure love is worth more to the Church than all other works (see Spiritual Canticle B, commentary on Sza.29). She goes on to quote again from John: "So it is of the utmost importance that our souls practice love much, so that consuming themselves rapidly, they scarcely stop here below and promptly come to see Jesus, Face to Face (Living Flame of Love, commentary on Sza.1:6).

She goes on to quote a verse from the Canticle of Canticles (5:2). She applies these words to Jesus. "Open to me, my sister, my well-beloved spouse, for My Face is covered with dew and my hair with drops of night". She goes on to speak of the Face of Jesus and seeing His suffering therein: "We want to wipe Your sweet Face". Thérèse had come to realise that there were people who did not believe. She says of them: "In their eyes You are still as if hidden: they regard you as an object of scorn". She calls them "our brothers". She recommends their consecration to her novices including Celine, in one of her poems "Heaven for Me" (PN32). Here she says:

> To bear the exile of this valley of tears
> I need the glance of my Divine Saviour.
> This glance full of love has revealed its charms to me.
> It has made me sense the happiness of Heaven.
> My Jesus smiles at me when I sigh to Him.
> Then I no longer feel my trial of faith.
> My God's Glance, his ravishing Smile,
>   That is Heaven for me!
>
> (PN32:1)

Jesus is 'hidden' in Heaven. In her act of consecration she says: "Your veiled Look, that is our Heaven, O Jesus". She makes an act of faith in Jesus' love which for now remains hidden.

The poem ends with a total reversal:

"I've found my Heaven in the Blessed Trinity
That dwells in my heart, my prisoner of love.
There, contemplating my God, I fearlessly tell him
That I want to serve him and love him forever.
Heaven for me is smiling at this God whom I adore
When He wants to hide to try my faith.
To suffer while waiting for him to look at me again
That is Heaven for me! ...

(PN 32:5)

Thérèse finds consolation in the night of faith in the total surrender of herself to Jesus. She consoles Jesus. She smiles at this God. From Thérèse we have a bright prayer to The Holy Face, composed in summer 1896 (Six, p.73). This was one of the prayers found in Thérèse's breviary after her death. In her prayer she says: "O my beloved, for Your love I accept not seeing here, below, the sweetness of your Look, not feeling the inexpressible kiss of Your Mouth, but I pray You to set me on fire with Your Love so that it consumes me rapidly ...."

The Last Days

During the year 1897 Thérèse's health declined. There were a few months of remission but this did not last. Finally she withdrew completely from community life. From July 8th, 1897 she was confined to the infirmary. A picture of The Holy Face that was in her choir stall was placed beside her bed. The Holy Face was something very close to her thought and theology. Mother Marie de Gonzague (Prioress since 1896) allowed Thérèse's blood-sisters to care for her during her last days. During this period Thérèse is tempted by suicidal thoughts. Pauline is in distress and prays before the crucifix that Thérèse not despair. She didn't. Guy Gaucher has this account of Thérèse's final hours: (Gaucher, Story of a Life, p.197f)

The following night, for the first time, the prioress ordered Sister Marie of the Sacred Heart and Sister Geneviève to stay with their sister. They took it in turns. Mother Agnès slept in the next cell. It was a bad night for Thérèse - filled with nightmares. She prayed to the Blessed Virgin. On the morning of Thursday, an overcast and rainy day, the three Martin sisters stayed with her during the community mass. She said to them: It is sheer agony, without any consolation.

167

All day she was gasping for breath but, to the surprise of all, she moved about, sat up in bed, which she had not been able to do for a long time. You see what strength I have today! She said. No, I'm not going to die! I still have enough strength for months, perhaps years!

Mother Agnès took down her exclamations in between her gaspings for breath, which was growing shorter all the time. If you knew what it is to suffocate! My God, have pity on your poor little child! Have pity on her!

To Mother Marie de Gonzague: O Mother, I assure you, the chalice is full right up to the brim! But God is not going to abandon me, for sure, he has never abandoned me.

In the afternoon after vespers Mother Marie de Gonzague placed a picture of Our Lady of Mount Carmel on her knees. O Mother, present me quickly to the blessed Virgin. I am a baby who can't take any more! Prepare me to die well. She was told that she was ready. Yes, it seems to me that I have never sought anything but the truth. Yes, I have understood humility of heart. It seems to me that I am humble.

Everything I have written about my desires for suffering. Oh! It is true just the same. I'm not sorry for having surrendered myself to love. Oh! No, I'm not sorry, on the contrary.

Sister Marie of the Sacred Heart was so upset by her godchild's struggle that she was reluctant to go back into the infirmary. Mother Agnès, for her part, went and prayed in front of the statue of the Sacred Heart, on the first floor, that her sister might not despair in her last moments.

About five o'clock the bell rang to summon the community quickly to the infirmary. The dying nun welcomed the sisters with a smile. She was holding her crucifix firmly. A 'terrible death-rattle' tore her chest. Her face was flushed, her hands purplish, her feet cold; she was perspiring so much that the sweat soaked through the mattress. Time passed. The prioress dismissed the nuns.

After seven o'clock Thérèse managed to say: Mother, isn't this the agony? Am I not going to die? 'Yes, my poor little one, it's the agony, but God perhaps wills to prolong it for several hours.' Well, all right! All right! I would not want to suffer for a shorter time. She looked at her crucifix: Oh! I love him! My God, I love you!

Her head fell back. Mother Marie de Gonzague had the bell rung again: the community returned very quickly. The kneeling sisters saw her face become once again very peaceful, her gaze was fixed a little above the statue of the Virgin of the Smile, 'for the space of a creed'. Then she sank back on to the pillow, her eyes closed. She was smiling. She looked very beautiful and had the appearance of a very young girl. It was about twenty past seven.

Thérèse had said in a letter to Abbé Bellière, "I am not dying, I am entering into life" (LT 224). Those who have been touched by her spirit can verify that!

Conclusion

"Why I Love You, O Mary" (PN 54)

In John Paul II's Apostolic Letter, 'Divini Amoris Scientia' (19th October, 1997) which declared Thérèse a doctor of the Church, he refers to the special place Mary, the mother of Jesus, played in the life and teaching of Thérèse. He spoke of "... Thérèse's wise delving into the mystery of the Virgin Mary, achieving results very close to the doctrine of the Second Vatican Council in chapter eight of the constitution Lumen Gentium and to what I myself taught in the Encyclical Letter 'Redemptoris Mater' of 25 March 1987". I had to smile when I read this. Thérèse with her spirit inspired prayer and intelligence saw what it took theologians longer to learn.

One could say that the Blessed Virgin followed her Son to the father by the little way of Spiritual Childhood. She was filled with the Holy Spirit and always said yes to God. She said yes to giving birth to the son of God. In her silence by the foot of the cross she silently consented to her son's self-offering. Pope John Paul II spoke of her 'kenosis of faith' at the foot of the cross (Redemptoris Mater, n18). This describes Our Lady's trial as she saw Jesus die. Péguy once said that Jesus took all the sin of the world on himself and Mary all the sorrows.

Charles Péguy (1873-1914) was a writer and poet whose life was marked by a battle of despair against hope. Mary came to embody for him true hope. In his poem 'The Portal of the Mystery of Hope' he describes Mary as the one to whom all the sorrow of the world has been entrusted. In the poem he speaks of a worried father who entrusts his sick children to the care of Mary.

> His three children in sickness, in the misery where they lay.
> And he had peacefully given them to you.
> In prayer he had given them to you.
> Placed very peacefully within the arms of she who bears all of the
>   world's sufferings.
> And whose arms are already so full.
> Because the Son has taken away all sins.
> But the mother has taken away all suffering.
>
> (Portal of Mystery of Hope, p. 29f)

Thérèse's trial of faith was one of compassion like Mary's. Our Lady sees the pain of every human being in the face of her son. Thérèse joins her in her ministry of prayer and compassion. Thérèse often confessed to Mother Agnes

(Pauline) that none of the sermons she had ever heard about Our Lady had ever touched her. The words she heard made the Virgin grandiose rather than truly great, ascribing to her extravagant privileges beyond those in scripture or in the teaching of the church. She speaks to Mother Agnes about preaching about Our Lady. She says:

> "How I would have loved to be a priest in order to preach about the Blessed Virgin! One sermon would be sufficient to say everything I think about this subject.
>
> I'd first make people understand how little is known by us about her life.
>
> "We shouldn't say unlikely things or things we don't know anything about! For example, that when she was very little, at the age of three, the Blessed Virgin went up to the Temple to offer herself to God, burning with sentiments of love and extraordinary fervour. While perhaps she went there simply out of obedience to her parents.
>
> "Again, why say, with reference to the aged Simeon's prophetic words, that the Blessed Virgin had the Passion of Jesus constantly before her mind from that moment onward? 'And a sword will pierce through your soul also,' the old man said. It wasn't for the present, you see, little Mother; it was a general prediction for the future.
>
> "For a sermon on the Blessed Virgin to please me and do me any good, I must see her real life, not her imagined life. I'm sure that her real life was very simple. They show her to us as unapproachable, but they should present her as imitable, bringing out her virtues, saying that she lived by faith just like ourselves, giving proofs of this from the Gospel, where we read: 'And they did not understand the words which He spoke to them,' And that other no less mysterious statement: 'His father and mother marvelled at what was said about him.' This admiration presupposes a certain surprise, don't you think so, little Mother?
>
> "We know very well that the Blessed Virgin is Queen of heaven and earth, but she is more Mother than Queen; and we should not

say, on account of her prerogatives, that she surpasses all the saints in glory just as the sun at its rising makes the stars disappear from sight. My God! How strange that would be! A mother who makes her children's glory vanish! I myself think just the contrary. I believe she'll increase the splendour of the elect very much. (DE 21.7.3)

When Thérèse was a child she was deeply unhappy at school. When Pauline joined Carmel things got too much for the sensitive child and she became very ill. Her father moved a family statue of Our Lady, called Our Lady of the Smile, into Thérèse's room. On May 13th 1883 the feast of the Pentecost, Thérèse turned toward the statue near her bed: "All of a sudden, the Blessed Virgin seemed beautiful to me, more beautiful than anything I had ever seen, her face radiated ineffable goodness and tenderness, but what pierced my soul was the ravishing smile of the Blessed Virgin" (MsA, 30r°). Thérèse was cured and she had a great love for Our Lady for all her life. When Thérèse was very ill towards the last days of her life she said during a brief period of remission: "The Blessed Virgin really carried out my message well; I'll give her some more. I tell her very often: 'Tell Him never to put Himself out on my account'" (DE 10.5.1). She did not want to be a nuisance! She also recalled an incident that occurred earlier.

During Matins. She spoke to me about her prayers of former days, in the summer evenings during the periods of silence, and she understood then by experience what a 'flight of the spirit' was. She spoke to me about another grace of this kind which she received in the grotto of St. Mary Magdalene, in the month of July, 1889, a grace followed by several days of 'quietude.'

"... It was as though a veil had been cast over all the things of this earth for me. . . I was entirely hidden under the Blessed Virgin's veil. At this time, I was placed in charge of the refectory, and I recall doing things as though not doing them; it was as if someone had lent me a body. I remained that way for one whole week."
(DE 11.7.2)

So Mary was Thérèse's constant companion in her journey to God. Mary's faith, hope and love were an inspiration for Thérèse. Mary personified Thérèse's little way. She had confidence in God and his mercy, she gave herself totally to God ('abandon') and by the power of the Holy Spirit her love embraced all people. She lived a poor and simple life doing God's will quietly and gently. This was Thérèse's great insight. Looking at Mary we see a living model for the little way. Thérèse was, in a sense, another Mary because she was close to Mary and was led by the Holy Spirit. The ones led by the Holy Spirit are the true-children of God. This is the essence of Spiritual Childhood.

Thérèse sensed the presence of Mary in prayer. She tells us the following:

> Sometimes when my mind is in such a great aridity that it is impossible to draw forth one single thought to unite me with God, I very slowly recite an 'Our Father' and then the angelic salutation; then those prayers give me great delight; they nourish my soul much more than if I had recited them precipitately a hundred times.

> The Blessed Virgin shows me she is not displeased with me, for she never fails to protect me as soon as I invoke her. If some disturbance overtakes me, some embarrassment, I turn very quickly to her and as the most tender of Mothers she always takes care of my interests. How many times, when speaking to the novices, has it happened that I invoked her and felt the benefits of her motherly protection! (MsC, 25v°)

In her beautiful poem, My Song for Today (PN 5), Thérèse reflects on time and eternity. Thérèse always believed that what counts for us is today, the 'now'. She said at different times "Let us see only each moment! . . . A moment is a treasure" (CG I, p. 558), "each moment is an eternity, an eternity of joy for heaven" (CG I, p. 587), "we have only one short moment of this life to give to God" (CG I, p. 882) and "Ah! Let us profit from the short moment of life . . ." (CG I, p. 1117), "I'm suffering only for an instant. It's because we think of the past and of the future that we become disappointed and fall into despair" (DE 19.8.10).

She begins her poem by saying:

> "My life is but an instant, a passing hour.
> My life is but a day that escapes and flies away.
> O my God! You know that to love you on earth
> I have only today! . . ." (PN 5:1)

Thérèse emphasises the importance of living in the present moment - not getting anxious about the future or too sad about the past. Jesus said: "So do not worry about tomorrow, tomorrow will take care of itself. Each day has enough trouble of its own" (Mt 6:34).

During this time, this 'today' on earth Thérèse prays to Mary to help her:

"O Immaculate Virgin! You are my sweet Star
Giving Jesus to me and uniting me to Him.
O Mother! Let me rest under your veil
Just for today"   (PN 5:4)

The symbol of the veil is a symbol for protection and giving shelter in the storms of life. In the Russian church they celebrate a feast-day in honour of Our Lady's protection - by using the symbol of the veil (pokrov).

This today leads to eternity. Thérèse says:

Soon I'll fly away to speak your praise.
When the day without sunset will dawn on my soul.
Then I'll sing on the Angel's lyre
The Eternal Today! . . "   (PN 5:11)

The icon of 'Our Lady of Perpetual Help' or 'Succour' played a part in Thérèse's devotion. She had a picture card of this icon in her breviary. She composed a poem in honour of the icon in March 1897. She is now suffering greatly. She says:

"When I struggle, dearest Mother,
You strengthen my heart in battle.....

Always, always, Image of my Mother,
Yes, you will be my happiness, my treasure.
And at my last hour I would like
To fix my gaze on you again.   (PN 49: 4-5)

"There is still one thing I must do before I die", Thérèse who was very sick said to Celine, "I have always dreamed of saying in a song to the Blessed Virgin everything I think of her" (PA, p. 268). She says yes Our Lady did suffer (DE

20.8.11). She wished to penetrate into the secrets of Mary's heart - to discover her way of love. Mary's humble love is wrapped in silence. For Mary, love is safer than knowledge. She is not afraid of what she does not understand. Whether in her attitude towards Joseph after the annunciation, in her at Bethlehem, or on the hill, Mary surrenders and abandons herself to God's will in silence. She lives in faith and by love. The end of her earthly life is immersed in a 'deep silence'. In the poem one sees Mary as mother and Thérèse as child. Thérèse was getting progressively weaker as she wrote the poem. Agnes had to help with the writing, the physical act of writing and the mixture of the styles of handwriting can be seen in the poem where Thérèse and Agnes wrote the words of 'Pourquoi je t'aime, O Marie!' (Why I Love You, O Mary). The first two Stanzas introduce the poem. In the second St.Thérèse says:

If a child is to cherish his mother,
She has to cry with him and share his sorrows.
O my dearest Mother, on this foreign shore
How many tears you shed to draw me to you! . ...
In pondering your life in the holy Gospels,
I dare look at you and come near you.
It's not difficult for me to believe I'm your child,
For I see you human and suffering like me .... (PN 54:2)

This is Thérèse's insight into how Mary caring as a mother for all her children. Thérèse goes on to meditate on Mary's life as we have it in the Gospels. For Mary:

"No rapture, miracle, or ecstasy
Embellish your life, O Queen of the elect!...." (PN 54:17)

It's by an ordinary life in Nazareth that Mary lives her life with God.

Thérèse also meditated on Mary's suffering on earth - no doubt thinking about her own struggles. She says:

Since the King of Heaven wanted his Mother
To be plunged into the night, in anguish of heart,
Mary, is it thus a blessing to suffer on earth?
Yes, to suffer while loving is the purest happiness! ...

All that He has given me, Jesus can take back.
Tell him not to bother with me.....
He can indeed hide from me, I'm willing to wait for him
Till the day without sunset when my faith will fade away.....

(PN 54:16)

Mary suffers because she loves much. She has a heart of compassion for her son's suffering and she sees all her children in her son. Thérèse says: "Yes to suffer while loving, is the purest happiness". This is what Mary did, Thérèse followed her in this.

At the end of the poem, Thérèse remembers the smile of Mary that healed her. Now she asks Mary to be gentle with her again as her life is drawing to a close. Thérèse says:

Soon I'll hear that sweet harmony.
Soon I'll go to beautiful Heaven to see you.
You who came to smile at me in the morning of my life,
Come smile at me again... Mother.... It's evening now!...

I no longer fear the splendour of your supreme glory.
With you I've suffered, and now I want
To sing on your lap, Mary, why I love you,
And to go on saying that I am your child! .....

(PN 54:25)

Bibliography

See also list of abbreviations used, page 2

and the comprehensive lists of selected works on Thérèse published in French before 1956 and after 1956 may be found in 'Aimer Jusqu'a Mourir d'Amour' and in Guy Gaucher's 2010 biography of Thérèse of Lisieux.

À Kempis, Thomas, *L'Imitation de Jésus-Christ* (English translation: The Imitation of Christ), Tours, Alfred Mame et fils, 1873

Arminjon, Abbé Charles, *Fin du monde présent et mystères de la vie future*, Chambéry, Paris, 1881.

Bellet, Maurice, *Thérèse et l'illusion*, Paris, DDB, 1998

Bernanos, George, *Diary of A Country Priest*, London, Boriswood, 1937

Bernanos, George, *Joy*, London, Bodley Head, 1948

Bro, Bernard, *Thérèse de Lisieux, sa famille, son Dieu, son message*, Paris, Fayard, 1996

Buber, Martin, *Eclipse of God*, New York, Harper Torchbooks, 1957

Buber, Martin, *Between man and man*, New York, Macmillan, 1963

Buber, Martin, *I and Thou*, New York, Charles Scribner's Sons, 1958

Buber, Martin, *Origin and Meaning of Hasidism*, New York, Harper Torchbooks, 1966

Buber, Martin, *Tales of the Hasidim I, II*, New York, Schohen Books, 1961

Bultmann, Rudolf, *Ginosko, TDNT I*, 689-719

Clapier, Jean, A, *Aimer Jusqu'a mourir d'amour*, Paris, Cerf, 2003

Clapier, Jean, *Une voie de confiance et d'amour*, Paris, Cerf, 2005

Conrad, Joseph. *The Heart of Darkness*, New York, Signet, 1950

Coste, Réne, *Le Gránd Secret des Béatitudes*, Paray-Le-Monial, Éd l'Emmanuel, 2004

Davies, WD and DC Allison, *Matthew*, London, T&T Clark, 2004

De Meester, Conrad, *Dynamique de la Confiance, Genèse et structure de la 'voie d'enfance spirituelle' de St. Thérèse de Lisieux*, Paris, Éd, du Cerf, coll. 'Cogitatio fidei', 39, 1969; nouvelle éd. revue et corrigére, 1995, Paris, Éd. du Cerf

Descouvement (P), *Sainte Thérèse de l'Enfant-Jésus et son prochain*, Paris, Lethielleux, 1962

Dupont, Jacques, *Les Béatitudes, III*, Paris, Gabolda, 1959

Frankl, V., Encounter and its vulgarisation, *Journal of the American Academy of Psychoanalysis* (1973), 1573-83)

Gaucher, Guy, *Je voudrais parcourir la terre*, Paris, Cerf, 2003

Gaucher, Guy, *Sainte Thérèse de Lisieux (1873 – 1897)*, Paris, Cerf, 2010

Gaucher, Guy, *Thérèse of Lisieux, The Story of a Life*, San Francisco, Harper, 1987

Guéranger, Dom Prosper, *The Liturgical Year*, Vadin, Paris, 1876

Heschel, Abraham Joshua, *Man is not alone*, Farrar, Strauss and Giroux, 2001

Heschel, Abraham Joshua, *The Insecurity of Freedom*, Philadelphia, Jewish Publishing Society, 1966

Heschel, Abraham Joshua, *The Prophets*, New York, Jewish Publishing Society, 1955

Hillesum, Etty, *An Interrupted Life*, New York: Owl Books, 1991

John Paul II, *Divini Amoris Scientia*, Rome 1997

John Paul II, *Mater Redemptoris*, Rome, 1987

Kavanagh, Kieran and Rodriguez, Otillo, *Collected Works of St. John of The Cross*, Washington, ICS, 1991 (incl. Ascent of The Cross, Living Flame, Spiritual Canticle and Commentary)

Kavanagh, Kieran and Rodriguez, Otillo, *Collected Works of St. Teresa of Avila*, 3 volumes, Washington, ICS, 1980 (incl. Interior Castle, volume II and Sr. Marie of the Angels, To the Visitation at Le Mans, 1893)

Kinney, David, OCD, (ed.), *The Poetry of St. Thérèse*, Washington, ICS, 1995

Lahaye, V, *Souvenirs d'un témoin aux cérémonies de Vêtre et de Profession*

Leclerc, Eloi, *Le Royaume Caché*, Paris, DDB, 1987

Leclerc, Eloi, OFM, *The Canticle of Creatures*, Chicago, Franciscan Herald Press, 1970

Levinas, Emmanuel, *Totality and infinity*, Pittsburg: Duquesne University Press, 1961

Marcil, I, OCD, *La kénose du Christ chez Thérèse de L'Enfant Jésus de la Sainte-Face*, Teresianum, Rome, XLVIII, 1997

Masson, Robert, *Souffrance des homes, un psychiatre interroge Thérèse de Lisieux*, Versailles, Saint-Paul, 1997

McCabe, Herbert, *God Matters*, New York , Geoffrey Chapman, Continuum Books, 1987

McIntosh, M A, *Christology*, Notre Dame, Notre Dame Press, 2000

Père Marie-Eugène, *Je veux voir Dieu*, Venasque Éd. Du Carmel, 1998

Paul VI, *Ecclesiam Suam*, Rome, 1967

Péguy, Charles, *The Portal of the Mystery of Hope*, Edinburg T&T Clark. 1996

Piat, Stéphan-Joseph, OFM, *Histoire d'une famille*, Lisieux, OCL, 1945

Rouiller, François, *Le Scandale du mal et de la souffrance*. Saint-Maurice. Editions Saint-Augustin, 2002

Sawyer, John FA (éd), *The Blackwell Companion to The Bible and Culture* (Alice Bach, Ch. 16: Film), Oxford, Blackwells, 2008

Sesboüé, Bernard, *Jésus-Christ, l'unique médiateur*, Paris, Desclee, 1988

Six, Jean-François, *Lumière dans la nuit, les dix-huit derniers mois de Thérèse de Lisieux*, Paris, Éd. Du Seuil, 1995

St. Thérèse of Lisieux, *Histoire d'une âme. L'autobiographie de Thérèse de Lisieux*, Moorzeke, Carmel-Édit, 1999

Thistleton, Anthony, *The First Letter to the Corinthians, NIGTC*, Grand Rapids, Eerdmans Publishing Company, 2000

Thomas-Lamotte, Pierre-Jean, *Guérir Avec Thérèse: Essai sur la maladie intérieure*, Paris, Téqui, 2001

Tillich, Paul, *The Courage to be*, New Haven, Yale University Press, 1980

Vatican II, *Lumen Gentium*, Rome, 1965

Von Balthasaar, Hans Urs, *A Theological Anthropology*, New York, Sheed and Ward, 1967

Von Balthasaar, Hans Urs, *Heart of the World*, San Francisco, Ignatius Press, 1979

Von Balthasaar, Hans Urs, *Mysterium Paschale*, Edinburgh, T&T Clark, 1990

Von Balthasaar, Hans Urs, *Prayer*, New York, Paulist Press, 1967

Von Balthasaar, Hans Urs, *Theo-Drama III, The Dramatis Personae: The Person in Christ*, San Francisco, Ignatius Press, 1992

Von Balthasaar, Hans Urs, *Thérèse of Lisieux, The Story of a Mission*, New York, Sheed and Ward, 1954

Films:

Apocalypse Now, Zoetrope Studios, 1979

Il vangelo secondo Matteo (The Gospel According to St. Matthew), 1964

La Vie en Rose, Légende Films, 2007

Medea, 1969

Mouchette, Argos Films, 1967

Oedipus Rex, 1967

Mean Streets, Warner Brothers, 1973

Thérèse, Xenon Pictures, 2006

Printed in Poland
by Amazon Fulfillment
Poland Sp. z o.o., Wrocław

56555368R00105